THE ADVENTURES
OF GEORGE PITTS

An Inmate with the Birdman of Alcatraz

George Pitts

ISBN 978-1-63525-339-9 (Paperback)
ISBN 978-1-63525-340-5 (Digital)

Christian Faith Publishing, Inc.
296 Chestnut Street
Meadville, PA 16335
www.christianfaithpublishing.com

Printed in the United States of America

A License to Steal

The Federal Government and the State of Texas Gave Me a License to Steal

It all started in 1959. I was twenty-two years old. Harold Vaughn, a buddy I grew up with in Buckner Orphans Home, Dallas, Texas, and I took off from Dallas for south Texas on a vacation. I was driving an old Hudson car. It had no brakes. I drove it 500 miles to Brownsville, Texas, without brakes. We stopped the car by turning off the keys, throwing the transmission in first, by opening the doors and dragging our feet on the pavement, and by hitting and scraping curbs.

Well, the party ended some 275 miles in south Texas at Edna. A policeman saw us scraping the Hudson against the curb and arrested us. The fine: $35 or three weeks in jail.

A few days later, a jailer asked me how much I wanted for a silver pitcher set, which was stolen. I said $35. We paid the fine and were released from the Jackson County jail.

Of course, without transportation, Houston, we have a problem. Solution: We slipped into the police car corral through an open gate, and with an extra car key, we stole the Hudson back, and away we went.

Nearing Brownsville at San Benito, we observed a police checkpoint in the distance. We were eating boiled eggs and drinking Gallo wine. Well, we were arrested and jailed in the Cameron County jail in Brownsville. Harold, my friend, was released, and I got sixty days.

Well, I'm in the jailhouse now. I'm in the jailhouse now.

In a large cell with about twenty-five Hispanics and one Anglo and myself, the problems started. Now, I get along great with Hispanics as I speak fluent Spanish. I later lived in Mexico for ten years. My wife is from Zacatecas, Mexico. However, unable to speak Spanish at that time, the other Anglo and I were considered intruders—gringos. The fight started. One tall Hispanic approached the other Anglo, swinging a belt with a large buckle. I warned him to duck. He didn't. *Wham!* A large cut appeared on his forehead. Blood flowed. Then the Hispanic approached me, swinging the belt. I ducked. He missed. Then all hell broke loose. Six Hispanics surrounded me, punching me out. I yelled, "Hey, one at a time! One at a time!" They retreated. "Who do you want? Who do you want?" they asked. "I'll take the dude who hit my friend." He was standing against the cell door. I approached him. My left arm has always been weak due to it having been broken three times. My right arm seems to have compensated; it was extra strong. I faked two left jabs to his stomach. Sure enough, he dropped his guard. *Wham!* I caught him in the jaw with a solid right hook. He fell like a sack of potatoes. Result? Six more Hispanics surrounded me, punching me out. "Hey, one at a time! One at a time!" I yelled. "Who do you want?" they asked. "I want the stocky, shorter Hispanic." We fought to a draw, and then I escaped to the cell door, banged on the door, and screamed, "Get me out of here! They're going to kill me." A jailer opened the door, raised his blackjack, and started to hit me. "Don't hit me! Don't hit me! It's their fault. They are beating me up." Thank god. He put me in an empty single cell.

Well, after a few days of boredom in the cell, I heard about the work detail for inmates who would be cleaning out the cemetery in Port Isabel. I volunteered. Once there at the graveyard, and when the guard turned his back, I jumped the fence and ran. After about four blocks, I came to a building with an apartment for rent. "May I see it?" I asked the landlady. "What's the monthly rent?" She said, "$300 a month." "May I move in right now and pay you Monday? I work for Brown Trucking Company on the outskirts of town." "OK," she said, so I was able to hide three days from the police.

By the way, I wasn't mentally ill. I didn't need a therapist. I was bored and had a character problem. I needed the Trinity—God the Father, God the Son, and God the Holy Spirit. My sister, Helen, of Tucson, Arizona, told me once, "Buddy, we come from a very dysfunctional family in south Texas." I replied, "No, we don't. We come from a sinful-as-hell family in south Texas!"

Well, to continue the story, I hitchhiked to Harlingen, Texas, and on Commerce Street, a deputy stopped and asked me for ID. I told him I had lost my ID. He said that I fit the description of one George Pitts, an escapee from a work detail at Port Isabel. "What's your name" he asked. "Loren Brodenbach," I said. "I'll call a deputy who recognizes Pitts, bring him over, and check you out." He came, and I went back to the Brownsville jail.

After serving sixty days, I was released. I hitchhiked to Phoenix, Arizona, where my mother and sister, Helen, were living.

I arrived in Phoenix in 1960, moved in with my mother and sister, sought employment, and got a job with Navajo Freight Lines as a billing clerk and general office employee. One of my duties was typing up company checks. These checks were on a Denver Colorado bank. Well, being bored with life in general, and not right with my creator, and lacking character, etc., one Saturday as I was working alone in Navajo's office, I typed up a bunch of checks in my name, left the truck line, and cashed three or four checks in various supermarkets in Phoenix. How dumb can one be? I used my own name on the checks and my own ID to cash them. Young people who are basically ignorant of the law do not realize the ramifications and consequences of their actions when they break the law.

Well, I took off in my green Nash to Nogales, Arizona, on another vacation. I bought $600 of new clothes and a Stetson hat in a clothing store there. After all, I wanted to make a big hit in Nogales, Mexico, with the ladies in the nightclubs. A beautiful young lady caught my fancy in one club. We got together and took off into the interior of Mexico. At the first immigration checkpoint, the officials wanted money, especially when they recognized the bar girl. They said they were real hot in the summer sun and needed money for some frescos (cold drinks). After paying the bribe, we continued on to Empalme, Sonora, near the girl's hometown. However, due to decreasing funds, I decided to turn around and head back to Baja California, and then into California. What a surprise I received in a motel in Mexicali when a preacher from Dallas, Texas, Jack Hyles, was preaching on TV from a Baptist church in El Centro, California. I had attended his church a few years earlier in Garland, Texas.

From Mexicali, I drove to Tijuana and then to Rosarita Beach, Baja California, where I decided to abandon my partner. Away I went into San Diego, California, where I commenced passing hot checks in various grocery stores.

I knew the police in Arizona and California would be looking for me, but little did I know that my hot checks were a federal offense—namely, the interstate transportation of forged securities. They had crossed a state line into Colorado. A few months later, I saw my wanted picture in a post office smiling back at me. I got a feeling of being wanted—by the FBI.

From California I returned to Phoenix and then decided to go back to Texas. I drove the long journey back to Dallas in my Nash. I slept in my car. The old Nash cars had seats that lowered backward, and one could make a nice bed in them.

Once in Dallas, a criminal has to make a living. Money is required in order to live. I hit a few grocery stores and passed two or three checks, and then it happened. Upon entering another grocery store, I heard the manager say, "And here he is now! You just stay put right there. I'm calling the police!" I didn't hang around much longer. I walked rapidly out the store and ran some six blocks and called a taxi. The taxi arrived and I asked him if he could drive down to Live Oak Avenue as I wanted to check on something. Sure enough, the Dallas police had found my Nash car and were beginning to tow it as the cab went by.

From there I decided to go way down yonder in New Orleans. I bought a ticket in Love Field in Dallas and flew to New Orleans. It was my first flight on a jet airplane.

Upon arriving in New Orleans, a sinner has to visit the French Quarter. Right? After consuming several bourbon drinks on Bourbon Street with a six-foot-tall bar-girl, I noticed I was almost broke. I was hungry, so I found a swanky seafood restaurant about a mile away. I deliberately sat close to the exit. I ordered $35-worth of delicious seafood—oysters, red snapper, shrimp, etc. Then I ordered dessert to get rid of the waiter, and I split out the exit door. I ran some six blocks to my rented room.

You say, "George, what a bum you were!" I agree. I was a bum. I'm now ashamed of that behavior, but I didn't care then. Was it mental problems? Psychological problems? Sociological problems? No! I had become a freethinker—more correctly termed, a free-stinker. There was no God, at least not in my life. If evolution was true and we came from monkeys, then why should I not behave like an animal?

Freethinkers, agnostics, and atheists try to separate morality from God. They think they can deny and reject God and still remain good and moral. One cannot do that. When one rejects and denies God like I did, morality goes out the window.

My problem was philosophical and spiritual, which resulted in my criminal behavior.

Now since Texas, God's country, was beckoning me, I prepared for my departure back to Texas.

First, however, I visited a novelty store in New Orleans and had a newspaper headline printed up in bold black letters: "George Pitts, Texas Rancher, Raises Hell in New Orleans." Later on in Texas, a couple of detectives were more interested in where I got these headlines than in investigating my crimes.

To save money, I hitchhiked back toward the Rio Grande Valley in Texas. I actually hitchhiked a ride on an airplane. I was standing on Highway 59, just west of Victoria, Texas, when a small airplane taxied up to a fence near me at an airport. I stuck up my thumb. The pilot opened the window, and I yelled, "How 'bout a ride?" He said to go in the terminal and buy a ticket, and he would wait for me. I bought the ticket, boarded the plane, and flew to Harlingen, Texas.

From there, I decided on a vacation on South Padre Island. I rented a nice motel room there and beachcombed for a few days. When my finances begin to run low, I hid some of the company checks under the mattress of my bed and traveled to San Antonio, where I continued to get ahead in business.

Upon my return to Brownsville, I called the motel on South Padre Island and asked them to bring my suitcase and clothes to a certain hotel in downtown Brownsville. They said OK.

Little did I know the maid at the motel had discovered the checks under my bed and had called the Brownsville police. What a surprise I experienced when an undercover police approached me in the hotel lobby, asked me my name, and arrested me.

Back in the Brownsville jail, I waived extradition back to Arizona and a US marshal returned me to the Maricopa County jail in Phoenix.

While incarcerated in the county jail there, I was charged with twelve counts of interstate transportation of forged securities.

I thought, *What do I do now?* I called my mother in Phoenix and asked her to get me out on bond.

First, I had an interview with a federal probation officer. When he asked me why I forged the checks, I decided to tell him the truth. I told him that the devil got in me. He replied indignantly that if I gave that explanation, my chances of probation would be nil.

Discouraged, my mother and I attempted to make bond. We signed a form giving the bondsman a two-bedroom bait house on a pier in a bay near Port Lavaca, Texas. I don't know if the bait house existed or not at that time. It might have already been washed away in Hurricane Carla of that same year.

Upon making bond, I immediately jumped bond.

I made my way back to Texas and found myself in Houston. Without money, what does a fugitive do? I bought an orange gas can and began panhandling money. "Sir," I said, "I'm out of gas. My car is four or five blocks over there. A few dollars would be appreciated." I collected about $90 in one hour.

One fellow who donated $3 had followed me. He told me to show him my car. I said it was six or seven blocks over. "Let's walk over and see it," he said. That did it. He dressed me down verbally and asked for his $3 back. Embarrassed, I gave it back to him, and that ended my panhandling career.

I recall traveling to Mexico City from Matamoros, Mexico, near Brownsville. I had false and incomplete ID. The Mexican immigration officer in Matamoros told me my ID was insufficient, but a tip of $30 secured my six-months tourist visa to Mexico City.

I visited the capitol and then the state of Mexico in the city of Toluca. I never will forget the sweet and cute little Mexican Baptist girl who invited me to her Hispanic church. I never went. She kept asking me why I kept drinking. I had rented a room from her mother. Little did she know that a fugitive's life is quite difficult.

I returned to Texas by bus. While hitchhiking outside of Del Rio, Texas, a local policeman pulled up and began to question me. He asked me my name. "Loren Brodenbach," I said. He asked my date of birth. I said, "December 1, 1937." He asked my father's name. "Jeffie Boone Brodenbach," I replied. He asked my mother's name. "Tennie Marie Brodenbach," I said. He asked me if I was in the service. "Yes," I said. He was suspicious as my ID was insufficient. "The US Navy," I answered. He asked me where I was stationed. I said, "San Diego." "Which base?" he asked. I said, "Camp Pendleton." That did it! Since he knew that Camp Pendleton was a marine base, he said, "OK. Out with it. What's your real name? We'll fingerprint you and find out." "George Pitts, "I said. I was placed in the county jail in Del Rio.

I tried making a run for it outside of the jail in a small fenced area. After a few feet, the policeman yelled, "Stop or I'll shoot!" I decided to hit the ground. Later, he told me I was wise to have surrendered as he had his .44 leveled on my back and was about to shoot.

The US Marshall again returned me to the Maricopa County jail in Phoenix.

Well, like the song says, I'm in the jailhouse now.

I learned rapidly in the university of crime—the local jailhouse. I asked some veteran criminals what I should do. One suggested I put on a nut act. Well, I did. I grew a beard, ate cigarette butts, and generally freaked out.

The other inmates agreed to cooperate. They hollered at the jailer to get me out of there. "He's crazy!" I was put in solitary confinement, and my theatrics continued.

I recall some problems that started between the whites and the blacks. The whites were calling out racial insults. The blacks set their blankets and mattresses on fire, and the smoke came into my cell under the door. "Hey," I said, "don't smoke me out. I didn't join in with those insults. Furthermore, I don't agree with what they said." Well, the smoke subsided, and I survived.

Upon being arraigned in front of a federal judge, I was disheveled and unshaved. I picked up a cigarette butt from the floor and ate it, and then I got dramatic. I threw a boiled egg over the bald head of the federal judge. It burst against the wall. That concluded my arraignment. I was remanded to the US Medical Center for Federal Prisoners in Springfield, Missouri, on a ninety-day commitment.

Arriving at the medical center, I underwent psychiatric treatment. They started out by putting me on Thorazine. It put me in the clouds. I spit it out. When I was interviewed by the psychiatrist, I would just sit still in a catatonic trance looking out the window. They put me in maximum security. When I cut my arm with a piece of glass, they decided I needed stronger therapy. I suppose I was not responding to the program, so the doctors sent me to the electroshock-treatment section of the medical center and changed my name to Freddie Kilowatt. They administered twelve electroshock treatments on the temples of my head. Before the shock treatment, they administered a drug and placed a wooden spoon in my mouth and shot the juice to me, Bruce. The idea behind electroconvulsive therapy is the shock temporarily obliterates the memory. A mental patient forgets what's driving him zonkers. This therapy has helped some patients. However, it terrified me. On the twelfth treatment, I decided to really freak out the shrinks. As I passed out, I hollered, "*Sho-who, sho-who, sho-who!*" I was imitating pigeons on my cell window. The doctors later told me about that.

Just prior to the thirteenth treatment, I felt a tremendous pain over my chest. This pain felt like the size of a silver dollar squeezing against my chest. The doctors thought I was having a heart attack and they, thank God, discontinued the treatments. An EKG later at the hospital revealed no heart problems. I was transferred back to maximum security.

In maximum, I'll never forget a black friend next door who committed suicide. His name was Hubbard. He cut his veins in his arms and bled to death.

I then decided to knock off my nut act. I wanted to get out of maximum security.

In 1962, a few days later, my mother came from Texas and visited me. "Bud," she said, "you're just as sane as I am. They told me you were crazy." Bernice, my sister, had given the doctors permission to administer electroconvulsive therapy. I told my mother to tell my sister to cease and desist and mind her own business.

I quit my nut act and started acting rationally. I had overacted and overplayed my hand. The doctors had me as crazy as a loon. They diagnosed me as schizophrenia undifferentiated—so nutty they could not even put their finger on it.

I tried to convince the doctors I was sane. I got on the basketball team and began playing. We played several colleges in Missouri. I was one of the better players. In one game, I made eleven straight baskets.

Finally, I was released from maximum security and placed back into population in an open dormitory. I responded to the program.

I asked the doctor for a job. They put me in the education department, which was right next door to the library. The Birdman of Alcatraz ran the library. He had been transferred to the medical center in 1960 when Alcatraz was closed.

I was stuck in Springfield on in indefinite commitment. I thought I would never get out. A jailhouse lawyer taught me how to file legal briefs and petitions to the federal court system. I started in the nearest federal district court and then appealed the petition to the Fifth Circuit Court of Appeals in New Orleans. I alleged that a mental patient who had not been convicted of anything should not be in a penal-type institution. I requested the charges be dismissed and that I be placed in a mental institution in Texas. Once, I received a letter from the attorney general's office headed by Bobby Kennedy. The letter was signed by Burke Marshall of the Civil Rights Division. In that letter, they agreed to drop charges against me and return me to an institution in Texas. I approached my psychiatrist on the dormitory. I thanked him for the treatment, etc. I told him that though I was still mentally ill, I now knew the difference between right and wrong, could assist my lawyer in my defense, and now could understand the nature of the pending charges, that is, the definition for legal sanity.

In 1962, I appeared before the psychiatric board of the medical center for my sanity hearing. I knocked off the theatrics and drama and tried to appear lucid and coherent. However, at the same time, I had to account for my erratic, bizarre, and abnormal behavior over the previous months.

I thanked the doctors for their treatment and especially their electroshock therapy. I told them that though I still had some mental issues, I really thought I was now legally competent. I explained to them I could now understand the charges, could assist my attorney in my defense, and that I could distinguish between right and wrong. These gurus of peace concluded I was suffering a delusion when I asserted my sanity.

The Criminal Rights Division of the US Attorney General's office had agreed to dismiss all charges if a Texas mental institution would accept me, so the nut board declared me legally sane but still in need of treatment. I agreed to return to the Phoenix court. Back I went.

In Phoenix, the US attorney agreed to dismiss charges contingent upon Texas accepting me in one of their hospitals. However, Texas balked on accepting me, claiming I could not prove residency. I had been quite transient in my lifestyle. Finally, after a stint in Phoenix, at the federal detention center in Florence, and the county jail in Tucson, I was returned to Texas and placed in the Terrell State Hospital in Terrell, Texas, some thirty miles east of Dallas.

After passing through the receiving unit, I was placed on the first floor of a building with other patients.

Then I made a mistake. Needing some exercise, I started shadow boxing on the unit. Apparently, I scared the fire out of some of the patients. They told the psychiatrist I was freaking out, so he put me in lockup on the second floor.

A few days later, the doctor visited me. I tried to assure him I was non-violent and was only getting some exercise. When he asked me how I was feeling, I said not so good. When he asked me why, I replied that a bird in a gilded cage is still an unhappy bird, and if he didn't soon give me some freedom—some yard privileges—I would really get sick. He then released me to the first floor and gave me yard privileges.

The next afternoon, I simply walked out of the hospital and ran east into a wooded area. I hid in some bushes and, later that night, began walking westward toward Dallas parallel to Highway 80.

It was very cold that March of 1963. The wind was fierce. About three miles west of the hospital, I came upon a little white wooden church. The door was open. I found refuge there from the cold and the wind, and went to sleep on a bench.

The next morning, I walked out to the highway and thumbed a ride to Dallas in a truck loaded with chickens.

The federal government and the state of Texas had given me a license to steal, so I took advantage of it. In Dallas, I was broke, so I continued to write hot checks. Back in the sixties, banks simply placed blank checks in the bank's lobby. I took advantage of their customer services.

When I called my attorney in Dallas, one Howard Law (of all names), he told me if I would surrender and return voluntarily to the hospital, he would get me out in ninety days.

A Methodist minister was called. He picked me up at the veteran's hospital in Dallas and away we both went back to the hospital.

Back in Terrell—what a surprise! I was placed in the maximum security ward—the incurable ward. Patients bayed at the moon at night like wolves—*Ah-uh-wo-wo-wo!* I had to get out of there—out of this hell!

They had me on the second floor. I checked out the grounds outside through the bars on the windows. I had a plan. I convinced an attendant to move me down to the first floor and allow me to watch TV in the lobby with other patients.

There was a security door to the lobby through which employees entered and exited. I noticed the attendants' shifts changed each afternoon at 5:00 PM. The attendant that came in at 5:00 PM was overweight. I sat near the door that afternoon in 1963, and when he came in, I ran out the door. I had an advantage over him. I weighed considerably less than him. He hollered at me and chased me. I sprinted some seventy yards along a cyclone fence and then turned sharply left as the fence turned. I ran some thirty or forty yards more and jumped over this eight-foot fence. Landing on the ground, I sprinted across the street, ran about a block, and hid in someone's garage.

About two hours later, when it was dark, I walked through town and came to a Nazarene church. I knocked on the pastor's door at his house next door, told him my name and that I had escaped from the hospital because I was not crazy. He promised not to call the police. I walked next door and sat down in his church.

Sure enough, in a few minutes, I heard the police car and saw its lights flashing. The pastor had lied to me. Fortunately, however, the cops came to the house instead of the church. That gave me time to run outside and two or three blocks over. I escaped. Suffice it to say, I never attended a Nazarene church after that experience.

A little later, I came across a house that rented rooms. I rented a room on credit. The next morning, I hitchhiked to Dallas.

In Dallas, my criminal career continued. I passed hot checks there and in other towns in Texas.

The fall of 1963 found me in El Paso and Juarez, Mexico. In Juarez, I rented a bar and went into business. I put the bar in the name of a local taxi-cab driver as an American cannot legally work in Mexico.

When American tourists and some locals started getting drunk, I simply placed half water and half beer in the beer bottles. After all, an entrepreneur has to turn a profit.

Why was I so crooked? I had bought into this evolution garbage. If we came from animals, then I would act like one!

I'll never forget an American fugitive in Juarez. His name was Richard. We became friends and began running together. He told me he and his brother had murdered a wealthy rancher in Yuma, Arizona, and that is why he had fled to Culiacan, Sinaloa, Mexico, before coming to Juarez. He told me there was a $10,000 reward on his head in Arizona to anyone who would turn him in. I didn't. After all, having gotten quite a criminal education in jail and in prison, one criminal must not squeal on another.

What an idiot I was. I should have called the authorities in El Paso about this murderer and had him arrested by the Juarez police and then collected my $10,000, about the equivalent of $40,000 in today's currency.

I also sold Richard my pistol, which he later wanted to kill me with.

A few days later, the *presta nombre*, the cab driver who helped me open the bar, told me Richard had stolen some of the bar's money. When Richard found out I was looking for him, he began looking for me. The taxi driver gave me a warning to watch out. I got the message. I bailed out of Juarez and moved to El Paso. The next day, the Juarez newspaper headlines read, "Asesino Peligroso Capturado" (Dangerous Murderer Captured). To this day, Richard, if he is still alive, probably thinks I put the finger on him. I should have.

My, how deluded criminals are! If the average crook would exert one-eighth of the energy he spends in criminal activities in legal pursuits, he would become rich legally. Perhaps it's the excitement of the chase or the adventure that motivates them.

In El Paso, I teamed up with another guy and showed him how to pass hot checks. I would go into a building that rented apartments and feign like I wanted to rent one. I would ask the landlord or landlady what the monthly rent was. If the rent was $200, I would take out a check for $300 or $400 I had previously typed up and ask the landlord if he could give me the difference. If the landlord hesitated, I would then borrow his phone and fake a phone call to someone. I would say something like, "John, it's Bob. I found a nice apartment. Bring over the U-Haul truck and furniture right now. I'm at 302 West Third Street." The landlord would then give me my change of $100 or $200. Then I would simply say I was going outside to await the truck and simply disappear.

After hitting up four or five victims, we were in another apartment house with the same scam when in walked the landlady's muscled-up son. He recognized the scam, explained that we were the ones passing bad checks all over the area, and said he was calling the police. I asked my buddy if we should take him on. My friend hesitated. He saw the guy's muscles. We decided to surrender. The police arrived and away to the pokey I went.

"You bum! You punk! You're not worth shooting," a detective on the fifth floor of the El Paso County jail told me. "You're going to get ten years in Huntsville!" Little did he know I had a federal and state license to steal.

The window was open. There were no bars on the window. I faked a suicide attempt out the window. I had one foot out the window and one inside. A detective grabbed me. "You're crazy as hell!" he screamed. I agreed (ha-ha).

When the authorities checked out my background, they dropped the forgery charges and placed me in the psycho ward at the Thomason General Hospital in El Paso.

In the psycho unit, I met Pam. She had beautiful eyes. She was gorgeous—tall, some five feet eight inches. We struck up a conversation and friendship, and soon I was composing a song for her. "My heart went *zam, wham, bam.* When I met you, pretty Pam. Yes, my heart flew when I first saw you." The life of a criminal gets lonely, and after all, Pam and I had something in common—insanity.

I told her I would call her as soon as I got out. She was going to be discharged soon.

I was on the first floor of the mental health unit. There was a large dining room. On one side of the ward was the kitchen. There was a large opening in the kitchen wall through which the kitchen employees passed food to the patients. We patients were lined up. On the left side of the opening was a door, solid at the bottom half and with a torn screen at the top half. The back door of the kitchen was unlocked. I saw my chance. When my turn for food arrived, I jumped through the loose screen at the top of the door and landed in the kitchen. I startled the employees. I raced out the kitchen door across the backyard to a low brick fence, which I scaled. The cook who was chasing me stopped at the brick fence. I ran about four blocks, went down an alley, and hid under an old Ford parked out back. I lay there about three hours. I then asked an old Hispanic man to call a taxi. The taxi arrived, and I escaped.

A few days later I called Pam. I told her where to meet me. Her dad found out about our meeting place. He called the cops, they arrested me, and back to the jail I went.

They sent me to the Big Spring mental hospital. After one day there, they released me. I hitchhiked a ride to Miami, Texas, in the Panhandle where I visited my mother.

Leaving Miami, I traveled to Laredo, Texas, and moved over to Nuevo Laredo, Mexico, to save money. I rented a cheap room in a motel on the Monterey Highway. Soon I found a girlfriend at the motel. By now, one could conclude that I had a woman problem. As I stated previously, a criminal and fugitive's life is lonely. We agreed to get married by the two laws—civil and ecclesiastical. My girlfriend wanted to get married in *blanca*—in a white dress. Away I went over to Laredo, Texas, to buy one. I bought a beautiful white wedding dress at a clothing store. Now, how was I going to get it past the Mexican customs upon returning to Nuevo Laredo?

I called a Mexican cab in Laredo and across the bridge to Nuevo Laredo we went. A Mexican customs official asked me what was in the box. "A wedding dress," I replied. "You can't bring that over here," he said. As I had little money to pay him a tip, I returned with the dress to Laredo. This time, I placed the dress in the cab's trunk and returned to Mexico. "Open the trunk," the customs man ordered. "You can't pass this dress," he said, so back to Laredo I went. What a game of musical chairs I played with that dress!

In desperation, I decided to swim across the Rio Grande River and smuggle it into Mexico. I walked about a mile from downtown Laredo and entered the river bottom at a shallow and narrow strip of the river. Then I heard the sound of a vehicle approaching. It was the border patrol. I hid the box in some bushes and waited. "What are you doing down here?" they asked. "Where's the box? What's in it?" "It's over here in the bushes," I replied, "and you won't believe what's in it." "What is it?" they asked. "A wedding dress," I replied.

They spent several minutes looking up "wedding dress" in their border patrol manual. When they couldn't find anything, they called their supervisors. Their supervisors couldn't find anything either about a wedding dress, so, laughing, the border patrol released me.

That did it. I developed a plan. I found a rooming house in Laredo. I feigned interest in renting a room. I asked to use the bathroom. I took off my pants and put the wedding dress on under my pants and shirt. Upon returning to Mexico, the custom agent asked, "Where's the dress?" "It's in Laredo," I replied. He ordered me to open the trunk, nothing. "*Pasale ustedes* [come on in]," he said.

At my fiancée's home, she and her family fell on the floor laughing as I disrobed.

The merriment probably decreased somewhat when I chickened out later, changed my mind about the marriage, and disappeared. At least they got a free dress and some laughs.

Another interesting episode occurred soon after that, on the other side of Nuevo Laredo. I rented a room in a motel and fell behind on the rent. I vacated the room and promised the motel owner I would return soon to pay her. A debt in Mexico is a crime.

A few days later, I showed good faith and brought her some money. Instead of winning her good will, she got mad and demanded the balance on the spot. When I advised her I had no more money, she threatened to call the police. I told her if she did that, I would bust every window in her motel. Then I ran some five blocks away. Well, here came the police van with about ten policemen inside and hanging on the outside. I ran into the middle of a block in which grew some mesquite trees. An old woman was outside washing clothes. She observed me curiously. All ten policemen began to surround me and slowly close in on me with guns drawn. What do you do now? Call on Charles Darwin for divine assistance?

The policeman nearest me, who saw me first, was shaking like a leaf—his hand with the pistol, that is. I thought, *He is accidentally going to shoot me because of his nervousness.* I told him in Spanish to be calm. I raised my hands. "Don't shoot, don't shoot," I said, "I'm surrendering peacefully." The other policemen grabbed me. One raised his nightstick to hit me. "Don't hit me. Don't hit me!" I cried. "Why did you run?" "Because I didn't want to go to jail." Apparently, the motel owner had told the police I was an extremely dangerous criminal.

They put me in the Nuevo Laredo jail with several other Mexican inmates and one American.

That night, one of the drunk Mexican inmates stole the keys to the cell block and about twenty inmates escaped. However, I, the classic escape artist, decided not to escape. After all, $30 would pay my fine and get me released.

Later that night, the police caught all twenty of the escapees, returned them to their cells, and beat the devil out of them with their nightsticks! *Wham!* One jailer hit an inmate with his black-jack on his arm and a bone, some four inches long, popped out. I told the American, "Watch out, here they come." When one of the police raised his nightstick to hit me, I said quickly in Spanish, "The American and I did nothing wrong. We did not escape. You hit me and when I get out of here, your brutality will be on the front page of the Laredo-Texas newspaper." The chief jailer then ordered his men to leave the gringos alone.

A few days later, someone loaned me the $30. I paid the fine and was released.

Another adventure found me in Houston, Texas, where I proceeded to buy a nice used Cadillac. I paid for it with a hot check.

Driving in style, I traveled to Del Rio, Texas, and crossed over to Ciudad Acuna, Mexico. I was sitting in a bar and talking to an American customer. He was drinking. I had brought in a Coca-Cola in my pants pocket. I bought a beer, went to the bathroom, poured out the beer, and poured the Coca-Cola into the beer bottle. I was a little crazy, but I wasn't dumb. I wasn't going to get drunk in a bar and have someone knock me in the head.

The American told me San Antonio was the capital of Texas. I said, "No, it is Austin." This started an argument. "Austin," I said. "No, San Antonio," he said. I suggested to the gentleman that we go outside to settle the problem. "If I knock you out, it's Austin," I said. "If you knock me out, it's San Antonio." Outside, the fireworks started. Conclusion: Austin was the capital.

Well, we Texans are noted for our rhetoric—our big mouths. I talked too much in the bar about my Cadillac. Here came the police. They arrested and jailed me for, of all things, a stolen car. What an injustice. I didn't steal it. I bought it with a hot check. The authorities in Houston had charged me with a stolen car violation in order to find me.

Well, the Mexican government couldn't even tolerate my presence. They kicked me over to the American side of the Del Rio–Ciudad Acuna Bridge and deported me as an undesirable alien.

Back to Houston I went. There I was placed in the Harris County jail where I continued to get sick—mentally that is. I told the inmates to cooperate and to ask the jailers to get me out of their cell block as I was crazy as a loon. The jailers obliged. I was placed in solitary confinement where I fell into a catatonic trance. While a psychiatrist examined me, I looked straight ahead without moving. He had some sense. He told the jailer I was faking. However, when my long nut record came in from Springfield, Terrell, and Big Spring, he had to go along with the program. I was sent to the maximum security unit at the Austin State Hospital.

Upon arriving there, one of my first questions to the unit's psychiatrist was if I was going to receive electroshock therapy. He said, "No, not at this time." What a relief. Mental hospitals at that time used electroshock therapy to control patients. I didn't want them to change my name to Freddie Kilowatt.

This was the only psychiatrist I met in four years that earned my respect. He said, "Pitts, according to this report, you were very sick in Houston. You've never been psychotic a day in your life. How long have you been faking insanity to beat criminal charges?" I remained speechless.

A few days later, a friend on the unit who worked in the kitchen told me the metal screws on the bathroom shutter securing the window were loose. Someone had loosened the screws with a Phillips screwdriver. He said if one used a star screwdriver, one could open the strong metal shutter and escape out the window.

Now the Austin Mental Hospital was maximum security. In 1964, it was a large, one-story rectangular building with a huge yard inside. It was about two blocks long and one and a half blocks wide. Patients going to different places in the hospital would exit their units and walk under a roofed walkway supported by round metal pillars. Occasionally, some patients would shimmy up the metal pillars and try to escape. They never succeeded. This place was almost escape-proof.

I decided to respond to the program. I felt my need of work therapy. I asked the psychiatrist if I could work in the kitchen. He said yes. I showed up the next morning with a Phillips screwdriver and a bag of used newspapers. The kitchen manager showed me how to operate the dishwashing machine. After about thirty minutes, I asked the manager if I could use the bathroom. She said yes.

The excitement started. I checked out the screws on the shutter. Sure enough, they were loose. I quickly removed them, threw down the screwdriver, and then tossed the bag of newspapers out the window to the ground below. I then climbed out the window backward, but a problem arose. With my feet hanging out the window some two feet from the ground, my belt snagged on the window sill. There I was, hanging by my belt between heaven and earth. I could neither crawl up nor go down. I gave a strong jerk and down to the ground I went. My right pants leg ripped from the hip to my ankle. I quickly tied my pants together with a shoe string, picked up my newspapers, and *shazzam*, I became the local newsboy.

I walked some two hundred yards down a sidewalk toward the fence that surrounded the institution. Several doctors and attendants passed by me on the sidewalk. I offered them a newspaper. They declined. They noticed my ripped pants. No problem. Most mental patients dress poorly.

I arrived at the cyclone fence and scaled it. In front of it was a drive-in restaurant. Upon seeing me, I could tell the employees were startled. I approached them and calmed them down. "Don't worry," I said, "I'm going back. I just wanted to buy an orange drink." They calmed down and served me.

With a drink in hand, I casually walked away down a sidewalk. After about two blocks, I noticed some tall sunflowers in a vacant lot. *A perfect hiding place,* I thought. I lay down, hid among these seven-foot sunflowers, and waited for the night.

Then the escape siren went off at the hospital. I soon heard police cars driving by slowly, looking for me.

I lay there all day. When it got dark, I walked to downtown Austin and rented a room at a cheap flophouse. It cost me $2 or $3. A man there loaned me a pair of pants. I spent the night there.

The next morning, I walked to the outskirts of Austin and caught a ride to Seguin, Texas. In Seguin, I hopped a freight train to Houston and visited a Hispanic friend. He had been in jail with me in Houston. He told me he thought he was seeing a mirage when I showed up at his house. I had promised him three weeks previously in the Harris County jail I would see him in about three weeks!

From Houston, I traveled to Laredo and lived in Nuevo Laredo, Mexico. That was in 1964. I met Edward Barosi there, an ex-policeman from Chicago. He had quit the Chicago police force and had come to Mexico. He said the Chicago mafia had threatened him.

Edward fell in love with a Mexican bar girl and later married her in Juarez.

We became friends and decided to move to Juarez. He and his fiancée went through Mexico on a bus. I traveled to Juarez through Texas via El Paso. Meeting up in Juarez, we made our plans. I told him the money was in Dallas and in Fort Worth.

Before we went to Dallas, Edward took off to Chicago to visit his parents. After two weeks, he returned in a brand-new 1964 Lincoln Continental. He told me he had bought it in Chicago with a bad check.

My reaction was to tell him to get rid of the shiny Lincoln as it would probably get us arrested. I was recalling my own sad experience with the Cadillac.

We drove halfway to Albuquerque, New Mexico, and ditched it on the side of the highway. To my chagrin, we discovered later that Edward's wealthy father had covered the check. Well, you can't win them all.

Arriving in Dallas and nearly broke, Edward and I decided to do my thing. We checked out a house with a room for rent. While the landlady was showing Edward the room, I was stealing money and her driver's license from her purse in the front room. Her first name was Billie. Later, I changed the name. I changed the name "Billie" to "Billy" on a typewriter, and using this forged name, I rented thirty black-and-white portable TVs from the Maverick Market chain in Dallas. We began pawning them in Dallas pawnshops, and then we went to Fort Worth.

With about ten TVs hidden in my station wagon under a blanket, we visited several pawnshops in Fort Worth. Then a police patrol turned on his lights and stopped us. I asked Edward if we should make a run for it or surrender. He was indecisive. Finally, he said not to run. We might get shot. In the sixties, police in Texas shot first and asked questions later.

We surrendered, were jailed, and returned to Dallas. We were remanded to the Dallas County jail. This was in August of 1964. We were placed on the fourth floor. Henry Wade was the district attorney. Bill Decker was the sheriff. Jack Ruby, Oswald's assassin, was on the fifth floor. Below us, we could see Deally Plaza where Kennedy was shot.

I served sixteen long months in that jail. I slept several months on the concrete floor.

Edward turncoated on me and told the DA I was faking insanity. He was released soon on bond. I remained in jail serving hard time.

The DA, who realized I was feigning insanity, kept me there deliberately until March of 1966. The charges were finally dismissed, and I was sent back to my old alma mater, Terrell.

Arriving at the receiving unit, I asked one of the patients who worked in receiving which unit I was going to. He said, "Chambers Hall." I froze. That's where they administer electroconvulsive therapy. I thought, *Over my dead body!*

Shortly, we patients bound for Chambers Hall were lined up, given a big white laundry bag in which to carry our clothes and things, and away we went toward this new unit. It was some two hundred yards away.

A big, black, heavy-set attendant was leading us. I lagged behind. About halfway to Chambers Hall, I dropped my laundry bag and sprinted some one hundred yards to a tall cyclone fence. The attendant was running after me and yelling for me to stop. I jumped on and over the fence at full speed, cut my hand on the barb wire, and came down on the outside of the fence. I lost one shoe. I ran east about a mile and collapsed in some weeds. Like I said, over my dead body.

I lay there all day. That night, I began walking west toward Dallas. I thought I was about two miles from Highway 80. I walked and walked and walked some more. Around midnight, to my horror, I walked right back to the Terrell State Hospital. I rubbed my eyes, slapped my face, and in soliloquy, I said, "Maybe I am nuts!"

No, I had walked in a huge circle half the night and had returned exactly back from where I started!

I took off west. This time, I stayed closer to Highway 80 so I wouldn't get lost.

Next morning, I got a ride to Dallas and then to McKinney, Texas. In McKinney, I was tired and hungry. I sought refuge in a Baptist church. The famous evangelist Lester Roloff was preaching. I explained my situation honestly to this man of God. He was understanding and did not call the police. The church gave me room and board for the night.

When Reverend Roloff preached that night, I thought maybe it was time I knock off this foolishness and get right with God.

One thing was for sure: all the psychotherapy and psychiatric treatment in the world plus painful incarceration hadn't changed me—maybe God could straighten me out and screw my head back on right.

The next morning, I got a ride to Oklahoma City. While crossing the Texas-Oklahoma line, I vowed never to return to Texas.

From Oklahoma City, I caught a ride to California and rented a room from a little ol' lady from Pasadena. Maybe in sunny Southern California I could find my true inner self.

The summer of 1966 found me in the Imperial Valley of California. In Calexico, I decided to go into business for myself. In a variety store, I bought five small transistor radios for $15 ($3 each). My, what a beautiful salesclerk was Mercedes Coronado, who sold me the radios. She later became my girlfriend. She was the sister of Coronado Aguayo, the number two man in the Mexicali police force.

I took the radios to my hotel in Mexicali to sell them. In Mexico in the sixties, the electronic industry was a protected industry. Bringing electronic items into Mexico was illegal. In fact, smuggling electronic items into Mexico was tantamount to smuggling drugs— punishable by five years in prison. As a result of this protectionism, Mexican radios, such as the Royal or Majestic brands, were three or four times as expensive as radios in the United States—thus my new business.

One day, while selling these small transistor radios for about $6 to $12 each near my hotel, a Mexican policeman stopped me and challenged me. "What are you doing?" he asked. "Selling radios," I replied. He asked me if I had my invoices. "Yes," I replied. "Do you have permission to work in Mexico?" he asked. "No," I answered. "You're in trouble," he said. "I'll have to take you downtown to the police station." At that, I removed Mercedes's picture from my bill-fold and showed it to him. He asked me if Mercedes Coronado was my girlfriend. I answered yes. He returned the picture to me and said to keep selling the radios and good luck.

A few days later, in a park in Mexicali, a newspaper man told me to watch out for Coronado Aguayo as he was involved in drugs. I kept that in mind, especially when Aguayo, Mercedes, the Coronado family, and myself went over to Tecate, Mexico, for a weekend out-ing. I remember Aguayo doing target practicing on large boulders with his pistol.

A few nights later, I was singing Mexican songs in a Mexicali piano bar. I was drunk as a skunk. I thought I was making a big hit with the Mexican folks, that is, a gringo singing Mexican songs. On one side of the piano sat Aguayo and his friend. The friend approached me. "Thomas," he said, "we know who you are. You just came here from El Paso, Texas. I believe you're a finger for the FBI. You better watch out!" As you're aware, most criminals are paranoid.

Though quite inebriated, I sensed the danger. I quit singing, bailed out of the bar, zigzagged four blocks, entered a small café, and drank several cups of coffee. I then went to my hotel, grabbed my earthly possessions and my radios, and caught a bus to Tijuana.

In Tijuana, I called Mercedes on the phone. She asked me what happened. I told her that her brother had threatened me in the piano bar. I told Mercedes good-bye and to look for another boyfriend. Love was great, but life was greater.

P.s Coronado Aguayo was killed a few months later in a shootout with the police in Sonora.

In Tijuana, I continued to expand my electronic business. I went over to San Ysidro, California, and began buying transistor radios from a Jewish merchant, Henry Bookspan. After a few weeks, I asked him if he would give me his source of supply of the radios in Los Angeles. He obliged. He sent me to TOPP Imports and Kay International in the City of Commerce. There I bought the same radios at a lower price.

My radio business in Tijuana really began to grow. I sold radios to every store in town. Also, I sold radios to every store in Rosarito, Ensenada, and Tecate. My sales pitch ran something like this: I would go into a bar with a radio playing. The bar girls would ask me to give it to them. I would decline. Then they would ask me how much I wanted for it. I would reply I was a broke tourist and had spent all my money in the bars. They would then begin making offers—$3, no; $5, no; $10, yes! I would say. The radio cost me $1.50 in Los Angeles.

I began buying portable radios—AC/DC, AM/FM. They cost me $7 or $8 each. I would sell them from $16 to $40. What a profit margin. These same Mexican radios would cost them between $40 and $65.

I would put some thirty radios of identical design and color in my car trunk. When a policeman on the street would see me with radio 20, he assumed it was the original radio 1.

One day, a Tijuana municipal policeman stopped me in the Zona Norte District in Tijuana, the bar area of the city. He asked me for my invoices. I showed them to him. He arrested me and placed dozens of my radios in his police car. I gave him $60, and he returned the radios to my car, and on my way I went.

One customer who owned a wholesale candy warehouse in the Colonia Independencia asked for one hundred portable AC/DC, AM/FM radios each week. I made $2 to $3 per radio.

I would buy the radios in Los Angeles, transport them to the border at San Ysidro, and among trees and brush in San Ysidro, I would hide them in my motor, trunk, and under the front and backseats. I always retained my invoices in case the cops showed up. Several times a redheaded San Diego policeman caught me hiding radios in my car in the bushes. He gave me several warnings. "George, someday you are going to get in trouble in Mexico." I usually thanked him for the warning and then I would advise him that it was not illegal to hide legal merchandise in one's car.

Tijuana, Mexico, is a free-trade zone, unlike other cities on the border. One can just drive through the border into Tijuana, usually without being stopped.

Little did I know my luck was about to run out. One day while delivering radios in the Zona Norte to a wholesale customer, a policeman detained me. A jealous merchant who sold Mexican radios in his store nearby had called the police on me. I offered the policeman $20. He refused. I offered $40. He refused again. I offered him $60. No. $100. No. I should have run. He was holding me for the federals.

The federals showed up and put me in the Tijuana jail, a real hellhole. I was in a cell block with about thirty inmates. The cell block was some forty-five feet by forty-five feet. The toilet was a ten-inch hole in the floor. You ate food if relatives or friends brought you something. The jail did not give you diddly-squat.

I had hidden thousands of Mexican pesos in my socks, the equivalent of about $700. Now what does one do? Federal authorities in Mexico do not take penny-ante bribes. They throw you in jail and ask for real money. In my case, they initially wanted $500, but when a friend of mine who visited me in jail told the police where I had other radios stashed, they asked for $1,500. I didn't have that kind of money.

I had perpetrated many escapes before—Port Isabel, three times from Terrell, one time from El Paso, and one time from Austin. I decided on the granddaddy of all escapes—from the Tijuana jail. Smuggling electronic items into Mexico at that time called for a minimum sentence of five years in prison.

I had a plan. I called Comandante Rodriguez on the phone. He was the head of Mexican immigration. His office was on the border with San Ysidro. I introduced myself. "Oh, yes," he said, "you're George Pitts, in for electronic items violations." I told him I had $700 in pesos hidden in my socks. I mentioned I was afraid the inmates would rob me if they discovered this money. I asked him if I came down to the border, would he safe-keep my money for me? "Yes," he said. I asked him if he would give me a receipt for the money. He said yes. I asked him several times if he would give me *un recibo* (a receipt). He assured me each time he would. I also told him I wanted to confess where other radios were stashed in Tijuana. I was taken down near the border, handcuffed.

I was placed in a government office some two blocks from the US border.

I was questioned for two hours by two detectives about my activities in Tijuana. They typed up the confessions (*declaraciones*). I asked them when they would take me to *la linia*, the border, to speak to Mr. Rodriguez. They said shortly. I asked them about the handcuffs. I said they embarrassed me. They said they would remove them.

Off to the border I went. The handcuffs were removed. An armed detective sat in the backseat with me.

Unlike today, the US-Mexico border at San Ysidro in the sixties was basically open. The American point of entry was on the east side while the Mexican point of entry was on the west side. The office of Mr. Rodriguez was in a small wooden building. I got out of the car and approached Mr. Rodriguez. Just as our hands touched in a handshake, I bolted and ran toward the San Diego police substation on the United States side. I figured the detective would draw his 44 pistol. Running north, I turned around, and sure enough, his pistol was leveled at my back. I didn't think he would shoot, and he didn't.

Many tourists entering Mexico were coming down the sidewalk. Had he shot, he probably would have hit innocent people, causing an international uproar.

I continued running. One elderly couple was coming down the sidewalk toward Tijuana. Upon seeing me, I heard her say, "Honey, let's go back."

Suddenly, *wham!* A Mexican customs agent tackled me. He had come from my blind side, the right side. Down we went to the concrete pavement. He grabbed me by my legs. I crawled forward, breaking his grip. There we were, both of us, crawling on all fours on the concrete pavement toward the USA. I won the crawling match. After some thirty yards, I fell into the loving arms of a San Diego policeman.

"What in the world are you doing?" he asked. "*Yo estoy pidiendo asilo politico*," I replied. "I am asking for political asylum." "Political asylum?" he asked. "You sound like an American to me. Are you from Texas?" "Yes," I said. "Please tell the officer to release my arm. He's breaking it!" "Release his arm a little," he said. "Thank you," I replied. "I needed that!"

The San Diego police put me in a small holding cell. Then a running conversation started between the Mexican and American authorities. The Mexicans sent word to me if I returned voluntarily to Tijuana, they would treat me real well. They would give me a private cell, three meals a day, color TV, etc. I told the San Diego police to tell them that unless they extradited me, hell would freeze over before I returned to Tijuana.

Then in came that redheaded policeman who had warned me previously. "George, I told you." "You were right," I said.

The San Diego police transferred me to the city jail in downtown San Diego, detained me two days, and then released me.

The following Sunday, I visited the large swap meet in National City, and who did I meet but my Zona Norte wholesale radio customer. "George!" he exclaimed. "How did you get out?" "I made bond," I said. That ended my electronics business in Mexico.

Later on in 1967, I received several traffic tickets in San Diego. I went downtown and spoke to the city attorney. When I showed him my nutty papers, he simply dismissed the tickets.

In 1968, while buying radios in the City of Commerce, I wrecked my Chevrolet Corvair. I was charged with no insurance, a violation of the financial responsibility law. I appeared in court in the City of Commerce. A somewhat arrogant and overconfident assistant prosecutor asked me how I pled. I hollered out not guilty by reason of insanity in front of some thirty defendants. "What did you say?" he asked indignantly. "Not guilty by reason of insanity," I replied. "You're nuts," he said. "Maybe you're right," I said. "Come with me and let's talk to the main prosecutor," he said. When I presented my mentally ill papers, the DA dismissed the ticket. After all, a poor mental patient like me didn't understand what was going on and wasn't responsible.

Finally, my conscience got the better of me. I was tired of faking it. Being legally a psychotic hurt my pride. I called my attorney in Dallas, Texas, and asked him if I could return to Dallas and have my legal sanity restored. He said yes, but first it was necessary to take and pass a psychiatric examination in California and in Texas. I passed these two examinations, returned to Dallas, surrendered with my lawyer, had a sanity hearing before a Dallas judge, was adjudicated sane, was processed, and was released. This was in 1969.

After actually getting some jobs in Texas and California, I moved to Imperial Beach, California, in 1972. I was delivering pizza for Caruso's Pizza in downtown San Diego.

A few days later, in a park in downtown Tijuana, I met my future wife, Soledad Aguilera, a gorgeous Mexican Marilyn Monroe. Light-skinned, blond hair, a slender figure, and a beautiful, humble spirit—it was love at first sight! We decided to get married.

As Soledad's father was a very strict Catholic, we decided to elope. She crawled out of her bedroom window there in Tijuana and met me at a grocery store three blocks up the hill. We eloped to Winter Haven, California, where we were married in September of 1972.

We were gone two weeks. Chole's (her nickname) family was very worried about her. Her large family consisted of fourteen brothers and sisters. Remember, we hadn't advised them about our eloping. Chole told me her dad had three pistols and two rifles, and he was mighty handy with a gun and a knife.

After two weeks, we showed up at Chole's house in Tijuana. I was concerned, of course. I didn't like hot lead.

"Chole, *hija*, where have you been?" her father asked. "Who is this guy?"

"Hello, *suegro*," I replied. "I'm your new son-in-law, *sea por bien o sea por mal* [for better or for worse]."

Well, I was accepted into this family of sixteen. What a relief.

Esteban, my father-in-law, was a potter. He had several pottery furnaces on his property in which the family made and sold pottery. However, the pottery business was slow in 1972 to 1973, so Estaban began smuggling illegal aliens from his home state of Zacatecas into California in his pottery truck. He would place the skinnier Mexicans in a large strawberry planter, and away he would go into San Ysidro, California, with a load of some ten to fifteen customers.

Alien smuggling was, of course, illegal then as it is now, but it was not considered a real serious crime, unlike today. The smuggler (*coyote*) could get three to six months in jail, and the aliens (*pollos*) would be detained one to three days and then kicked back to Mexico.

Here I was basically unemployed. I was more of a character than one having character. I was approached many times by campesinos from Zacatecas pleading for me to take them to Los Angeles. Being quite materialistic, I finally succumbed to temptation, especially when I noticed the one-thousand-peso notes (about $80) they hid in the soles of their shoes. I asked them why they hid money in their shoes. They said that if the border patrol found the money on their persons, they would be flown to the interior of Mexico, but if they found no money, they would shortly send them back to Tijuana, and then they would return the following night to the USA.

I repeat, I yielded to temptation. At that time, I was like the evil judge in the New Testament. I regarded neither man's laws nor God's.

Away to downtown San Diego I went looking for a guide, a coyote, to bring over two clients.

One Antonio Ortiz from Jalisco state was sitting on a bench at a bus stop. Conversation ensued. Chole was present with me. I told Antonio I was looking for a guide to jump the border near the airport in Tijuana, to enter Otay Mesa, and bring two customers some six miles to a church in east Chula Vista on Telegraph Canyon Road. I asked him if he could do it. He replied, "*Sí, sí.*"

I took him in my green Volkswagen bug out to Telegraph Canyon Road in Chula Vista to scout the area. Then I took him out to Otay Mesa Road to check out the area near the border. Then we cased out the area in Tijuana near the airport. Now we were ready for action.

That night, I dropped Antonio and the two pollos off in Tijuana near the airport, and departed. The next day, there they were at the designated spot and away I went to Los Angeles, 125 miles north.

At that time, there were two border patrol checkpoints north of San Diego. There still is today—one at San Clemente on I-5 and the second one at Temecula on the old Highway 163 (I-15 today).

I chose the Temecula route because there was a highway bypassing the checkpoint on the east side by way of Pala, California.

I zipped around the checkpoint, passed through Riverside, got on I-10 West, and arrived in Los Angeles. They paid me $400. I almost fainted—$400 in four hours of work is pretty good money.

I returned to Tijuana, paid Antonio $50, and planned my next move.

Estaban had built several rooms, kind of a court, on his property. Some ten customers from Zacatecas were roomed there and awaiting their ride north. I obliged.

In a few weeks, the business was prospering. I decided to upgrade the operation, so I rented a U-Haul van. After all, the U-Haul motto at that time was "Adventure in hauling!" First I took three or four to Los Angeles, then six, and soon up to fifteen people. I usually used the Pala bypass, but sometimes I drove all the way to Blythe, California, near the Arizona border, and then on I-10 West to Los Angeles. Money rolled in by the thousands. I had struck gold.

In 1973, I recall going to Hines Pontiac in San Diego to buy a large car. A large two-tone four-door Dodge Polara caught my attention.

The car salesman was in front explaining all about the V-8 engine, but I was at the back examining the large trunk. "It's a V-8," he said. *I can get seven to eight skinny people in the trunk,* I thought. I bought the Dodge Polara.

The business flourished, and my bank account in the Banamex Bank in Tijuana increased rapidly.

Chole's uncle, Santos Lorenzano, at that time was probably the biggest alien smuggler in Tijuana. He lived four blocks up the hill from Chole's house. We started working with him. He usually had twenty to thirty customers in his home waiting for their ride north.

Money flowed in. We soon controlled two hotels in downtown Tijuana. We had dozens of people waiting for us all the time. Everyone wanted to go with me and Chole because I was respectful of girls and women. I would give them breakfast at Jack-in-the-Box. I always allowed ample oxygen in the trunk of my car. I never in three years of smuggling lost a customer. I would open the windows on both sides of the car. I had cut two holes about six inches in diameter in the back of the car where speakers are mounted. Over these two holes I placed two round silver speaker lids with perforations. As I drove north with up to seven clients in the trunk, I would uncover the holes with a long metal rod, and put the speaker covers to one side. If I saw a border patrol or a policeman, I would simply gently move the speaker covers back over the holes from my position in the front seat with the long metal rod.

The corporation continued to grow. I recall bringing in people from Central America, Ecuador, Argentina, etc. I put several on airplanes to New York and Boston at the Los Angeles International Airport, including one student who attended Boston University.

I had many close calls. One time in 1974, Antonio brought over about ten people. However, he was not in the designated spot. That morning, I searched for him and his people. I finally found him and his group about a fourth of a mile away. I asked him why he was over there. He said he and his group had to run and hide from a border patrol.

Antonio and his ten customers were hiding right next to a tomato farm where several farm workers were picking tomatoes. I tried to figure out how I could get them out of there without raising suspicion on the part of the farm foreman. I decided to pose as a border patrol agent. In Chula Vista, I rented a large green car. I bought a pair of green pants, a green shirt, and a green cap at a used thrift store. Dressed in green, I drove back up to the farm gate and hollered at the foreman, "Come here!" "Yes," replied the foreman. "United States Immigration and Naturalization Service," I said. "There're several illegal aliens hiding nearby. I'm going to bust them. By the way, do all of your workers have papers?" "Yes," he said. I questioned one to two of his workers, "Your papers please." The two obliged and showed me their papers.

I drove over to where Antonio and his people were hiding. I told him, "They think I'm the border patrol. I'm going to feign arresting you guys. Play along. I'm going to punch a few of you as you get in the car." They approached the car. I shoved some of them roughly. They all got in, and away we went to Los Angeles.

Another close call occurred in 1974 east of San Diego, between Borrego Springs and Salton City. I was driving along merrily in my yellow Ford Maverick heading east when I was surprised by a mobile checkpoint. It was about a fourth of a mile away. I had two in my trunk. I told them a border patrol checkpoint was in front. I instructed them not to make a sound. I gently covered up the holes at the back of the car with the long narrow metal rod. Arriving at this surprise checkpoint, I was greeted with the US Immigration and Naturalization Service greeting. "Good afternoon," I said. They looked inside the car and said, "Have a nice day." On I went.

By the way, the reason I never lost a customer in the trunk is because I always designated one person in the trunk to communicate with me. Every two to three minutes I would holler *"Como estan?"* He would reply, "OK." I told him if he didn't answer, I would stop and open the trunk immediately.

Perhaps the closest call and the most dramatic and dangerous occurred one night in 1975 about midnight. I was trying to circumvent the Temecula checkpoint just north of Pala. I had fifteen of Don Santos's customers in a U-Haul van. I had them hidden and covered under a large flattened refrigerator cardboard box. I was some three miles north of Pala. I was driving along, happily singing in Spanish and telling my fifteen pollos what a great coyote I was. They agreed I was wonderful. Suddenly, to the right about one block out, a car's light came on. As I passed by, I saw the border patrol seal on the door. *What do I do now?* I thought. I cried, "Border patrol behind us! Good-bye!" I stopped the van on the left shoulder, put it in park, and ran west. I jumped a ditch and split. After running straight west about forty yards, one shoe came off. This caused me to turn left, and I ran another forty yards back south parallel to the highway. The night was pitch-black. I was fortunate I didn't run right smack into a tree. Suddenly, I fell into a small arroyo. Down I went into some brush. I lay still. The border patrol agents were cursing and running northwest up a hill. I could see the lights of their flashlights. I figured I had one in a hundred chance of escaping. I then heard rustling in the grass nearby. I thought it was the border patrol, but, no, just some rats or something. I lay still for one hour. The border patrol left. Then it dawned on me, if they bring out a dog, they'll find me in fifteen minutes.

I got up and started walking south. I found a creek and followed the creek bed toward Pala, an Indian town three miles away. I arrived in Pala about five in the morning. An Indian man was warming up his car. I approached him. "Good morning," I said. "What happened?" he asked. I told him I wrecked my car three miles north and asked if I could pay him $100 to take me to San Diego. He agreed. I had escaped. What luck, or perhaps a divine miracle.

Another interesting adventure occurred that even today I don't believe it happened. In my Dodge Polara with the extra-large trunk, I decided to take Mario Aguilera, Chole's uncle, and his five friends—a total of six—to New York City from San Diego. Like the TV commercial, I wanted to see the USA in my Chevrolet—no, I mean my

Polara. I was becoming overambitious. I was going to drive three thousand miles with six in my trunk!

We dressed all six in nice suits and ties, and went toward Arizona. Three were in the back of the car and three were in the trunk. We rotated them. At Lake Havasu, Arizona, we stopped at the agricultural inspection station. The ag-inspector shocked me. "Open the trunk," he said. "I'm sorry, sir," I replied, "I've lost the keys to the trunk, but I only have this apple"— which I was eating. "Good day," he said.

We continued on east, getting our kicks on Route 66. Our daughter, Diana, age one, was with us. In northern Arizona, we decided to see the Grand Canyon. After depositing the six in a wooded area, we enjoyed the splendor of the Grand Canyon.

Onward we went on 66 East. In St. Joseph, Missouri, we deposited the six in a wooded area. We gave them food, water, and some blankets, and instructed them to meet us there the next morning. Chole, Diana, and I, of course, stayed in a nice motel.

The next morning, low and behold, the six were not there. We found them several blocks away. I asked them what happened. I asked them why they moved. Mario replied, "A ten-foot animal came near us last night and scared the fire out of us!"

We traveled on. I thought that the arch at St. Louis was a bridge at first.

On into Kentucky we went, and then Ohio, Pennsylvania, and then New York.

I called the deputy sheriff in Goshen, New York, some thirty miles north of New York City. "I brought your six workers," I said. "Do you have the $4,000?" "Yes, I do," he replied. "You're not going to put us in jail are you?" "Of course I'm not. I'm a man. My word is good. My father, George, needs them in his orchard." We arrived at Goshen, collected the four grand, and went back to New York City to see the Statue of Liberty. Then we returned to San Diego.

On the way back, I stopped in a small town in the Panhandle of Texas to visit my aunt Slater, my mother's sister. She was a devout Christian. She told me, "Let me tell you what makes me tick." She gave me the message of Jesus Christ. I left in tears!

Returning to San Diego, we continued our illegal enterprise. Now, of course, I was wanted by the immigration authorities as they had found out I had rented the U-Haul van they confiscated that night near Pala. I worked right under their noses in San Diego for about two more years.

In the fall of 1975, Chole and I visited her ranch, an *ejido*, in Zacatecas. Ranches, or *ejidos*, in Mexico have hundreds and thousands of people. An *ejido* is government-owned, but Mexican citizens are allowed to live on the land if they work it.

I played first base on the ranch's baseball team. I batted cleanup as I was a home-run hitter. The players and the entire ranch of two thousand people treated me like a white Pancho Villa. After all, treat George and Chole really well and maybe George will take you to Los Angeles *de okies* (free of charge). Maybe Esteban, George's father-in-law, may give you free room and board in Tijuana.

Well, an interesting thing happened on the way to the office. Understand, I was there passing out business cards of the two hotels in Tijuana—trying to drum up a little more business when I came down with a terrible sickness. It was an abominable abdominal infection. I was dehydrated, was vomiting, and had diarrhea—*la venganza de Montezuma*—the revenge of Montezuma. It was either a result of eating green peanuts or contaminated chorizo. Although I was a strong athlete then, I was sinking fast. In a hotel in Jerez, Zacatecas, I steadily weakened from around 8:00 PM until midnight. At 9:00 PM, I cried, "Help me, God!" Then the subsequent pain of conscience hit, which said, "Live like the devil, violate the laws of both countries, and then you cry out to God." At 10:00 PM, I prayed again, "Help me, God." Again the condemned conscience. At 11:00 PM, again the cry and again the pained conscience. At twelve midnight, it suddenly dawned on me if I repent of my sin and invite Jesus to come into my heart, this might open the door for God to hearken to my prayer for help. My old mother, now deceased, had taught me as a child that God would not hear sinners who would not repent, but was rich in mercy to those who would. The spiritual transaction took place quickly, in about fifteen seconds. I said, "Forgive my sins, Jesus, and come into my heart and help me in this sickness. Amen."

The next morning, I drug down to a clinic where they administered antibiotics and gave me glucose intravenously. In one hour, I had almost recuperated.

The next day, I went back out to Chole's ranch with a Bible in my hand. "Hey, George," my friends said, "come over and have a beer. Tell us some dirty jokes. Want to go see some girls in Jerez tomorrow? What's that in your hand?" "A Bible," I said. "Friends, you and I have come to a parting of the ways. You hypocrites, you go to mass each Sunday, do the sign of the cross regularly, wear crosses, and kiss a plastic baby Jesus at Christmas. You're religious as the devil. Juan, you have three women. Tomas, you beat me out of two thousand pesos. Rogelio, you're on drugs."

"George, *que tienes*?" they asked. "What's wrong with you?" "I've invited Jesus into my life, and he is a much better friend than you fair-weather cats."

Suffice it to say, I lost all my fair-weather friends. I returned to Tijuana.

One of Esteban's clients asked me how many I had in the trunk of my car. "Six," I replied. "Six?" he asked. "Yes, six Bibles."

We returned to our mobile home in Chula Vista. I started attending a small Hispanic Baptist church in San Ysidro and started discussing the Bible with my Catholic wife. "George," she said, "you have your religion and I have mine."

I consulted a lawyer, and he arranged for me to surrender at the Metropolitan Federal Detention Center in downtown San Diego.

I was incarcerated. I immediately started evangelizing the inmates. The cell block held about sixty prisoners. Some were in for very serious crimes, such as bank robbery, etc. About half of these inmates converted to Jesus Christ. I'll never forget one bank robber who invited me into his cell. "George," he said, "I don't have what you've got, but you've got something. Tell me about God."

I had twelve felony counts against me. When I went to court, I pleaded guilty to three misdemeanors, received ninety days, served my time, and went home.

Some of the more skeptical inmates called my conversion a jailhouse conversion and that I would shortly be smuggling more illegal aliens. How surprised they were when the chaplain of the detention center invited me two months later to speak to the inmates.

I needed to get my wife, Soledad, converted to Christ. She was a very devout Catholic. She told me she had her religion and I had mine, and to leave her alone. I replied that in the New Testament, it says that not only is Jesus our savior but the savior of the whole world (1 John 2:2). This argument, "I've got mine and you've got yours," held no water.

We fought like dogs and cats for three months and then, like cats and dogs, fought for another three months. Frustrated, I quit preaching to her. I began praying for her. I went over to Tijuana and bought her a Catholic Bible, which, in the New Testament, is basically the same as the Protestant Bible, with twenty-seven books.

One night in the summer of 1976, while praying, God seemed to give me peace about my wife. The next morning, she said, "George, I want what you have. You are so different than before. You're more patient with Diana [our daughter]."

Surprised and cheered, I began a theological discourse from Genesis to Revelation, long and drawn-out. This only confused her. Then it happened—I stumbled across Romans 5:1, "Therefore being justified by faith, we have peace with God through our Lord Jesus Christ." "What does this verse mean?" she asked. I explained that *justified* was a legal term meaning "just as if you had never sinned," and that one is justified through faith—not by works or baptism or human effort. One would have peace of mind through our Lord Jesus Christ, not through Mary, the priest, the pope, or the church—neither Catholic nor Protestant. She saw the truth, and her conversion was dramatic. She kneeled on the floor of our mobile home in Chula Vista and prayed to God. Down came the tears and then her makeup. She stood up claiming God's salvation.

She was baptized in the Lighthouse Baptist church in San Diego that same month.

We attended that church several months, growing in the grace of God and studying the Bible. We also actually kept the church from closing down by loaning the pastor several thousand dollars, which alleviated a financial crisis. This church, the Lighthouse

Baptist Temple, is now a large church in Lemon Grove, California, pastored by Doug Fisher.

Now, as Christians with lots of money in the bank in Mexico, what do you do with the illegal money? Should we give it to the IRS or to the US Immigration Service, or should we return to Mexico as missionaries and give it back to the people it came from? After consulting with our pastor and praying about it, we decided to go to Mexico as missionaries and give the money back to the Mexican people.

In the summer of 1976, we sold our mobile home in Chula Vista, gave away most of our furniture to our pastor and members of our church, bought a 30-foot Prowler travel trailer, and took off to Mexico as missionaries. We drove east on Interstate 8 toward Arizona in our Dodge Polara, pulling the travel trailer. At Jacumba, some seventy miles east of San Diego, we almost got out of control descending down a steep grade. Fortunately, I had the good sense to throw the transmission into a lower gear. We recovered and on we went. We crossed over into Mexico in Sonoita, just west of Nogales. We stopped to obtain my six-months tourist visa. I received it, and then Chole started crying. A drunken Mexican immigration officer had confiscated her border crossing card and refused to return it. He was asking for a bribe. I told his supervisor I would report it to higher-up officials if it wasn't returned immediately. He complied and returned it to her. Chole stated right then that though she loved the Mexican people, the Mexican culture, and her relatives, she no longer wanted to be a citizen of Mexico.

By the way, the Mexican authorities in Tijuana were no longer looking for me as the escape charges of 1968 were *archivado* (dropped) in 1975.

On south to Hermosillo, Sonora, we went. In that town, I was given permission to preach to the inmates in a Mexican prison.

The next day, I met a Mexican Baptist pastor at a Baptist church in this town. I told him I would be willing to visit in his town and invite people to his church. He asked me where I was from. I told him from California. He told me to go back to California. Mexican people are very proud of their heritage, are very independent, and are very nationalistic. Many of us gringos are viewed in Mexico with suspicion for many reasons, some being historical, that is, the Mexican war of 1850 in which Mexico lost much of its land—California, Arizona, New Mexico, Colorado, etc. Besides all this, we Americans were not exactly invited in to the Port of Veracruz in the early 1900s.

From Hermosillo, we traveled on south to Culiacan, Sinaloa, the bread basket and drug capital of Mexico.

I commenced preaching in a park in the downtown area of this city. I was sizzling. As I preached in Spanish, two armed policeman approached. "Now you've done it," Chole exclaimed. We thought they were going to arrest me as religious activity in the open air is prohibited in Mexico. But, no, they drew near, listened, and suddenly removed their pistols, knelt down, and invited Jesus into their hearts!

From Culiacan, we went on south through Mazatlan, through Guamuchil, and stopped at a small town called Alway. There we met a one Pastor Rocha who pastored a small Baptist church. He agreed to let me preach a revival at his church. I jumped on top of his Volkswagen van with a bullhorn and invited people all over this town to Christian services. Some five hundred people attended each night. Many made decisions for Christ.

On the last night there, some wild drunks were playing loud music and shooting their pistols in the air some two blocks away. I didn't realize they were drug traffickers. In my sermon, I shouted out, "If you're selling marijuana, you ought to be arrested! If you're selling hard drugs like heroin or cocaine, you should be shot!" God protected me. In spite of myself, nothing happened.

We left our travel trailer there and drove down to Tapacula, Chiapas, on the Guatemalan border. When we returned a few weeks later, we learned that three of these drug traffickers had been killed in a shoot-out with police in the Sierra Madre Mountains of Sinaloa. God had protected me.

My attitude in my preaching was this: Since I had risked my life smuggling illegals and basically living for the devil, why not be bold for God—why not risk my life for a righteous cause?

Later on, some more seasoned missionaries counseled me to calm down, to use discretion and wisdom. To this I replied I thought they were afraid and just wanted to save their own skin. They quoted me the verse, "Be ye therefore wise as serpents and harmless as doves," (Matthew 10:16b) to which I rebutted, "Be strong and of a good courage; be not afraid" (Joshua 1:9). So be it.

Arriving in Tapacula, Chiapas, I wanted to visit a preacher friend in Guatemala. I had met him in San Diego earlier—one evangelist, Hugo Avila. I wanted Chole and Diana to go with me, but the Mexican immigration told me they would not be allowed to return to Mexico, so they stayed in a hotel in Tapacula until I returned.

I got my tourist card from the Guatemalan immigration officer just south of Tapacula. When I took out a twenty dollar bill, he asked me what I was doing. I replied that in Mexico, a tip was customary. He said, "Put it back in your billfold. You're not in Mexico."

How beautiful and clean were the highways in Guatemala. The fence posts were all whitewashed, and instead of Pemex gas stations in Mexico, there were various American gas stations.

I arrived at Huehuetenango at Hugo Avila's house. Well, what a diet. Bananas for breakfast, stewed bananas for lunch, fried bananas for supper, and a banana snack before bedtime—thus the old American song, "Yes, we have no bananas because they have no bones."

In Huehuetenango, I began evangelizing. I asked almost every Guatemalan I met if he was sure he was going to heaven if he died today. They were very receptive to the Gospel message as they were in mourning. In that year, 1976, thousands had been killed in a strong earthquake. My second question was, if I could show them from the Bible how to be saved, would they do it? Would they accept Christ? Many said yes. They nicknamed me *pajarito spitz*, a local bird—a kind of play on my last name, Pitts. They said I chattered like a bird.

One day, while preaching in a bus in Quezaltanango, a drunk began mocking me and insulting the Bible. Some undercover police officers entered the bus, told him to shut up and be respectful to tourists, and to not mock the Bible. They arrested him and carried him away feet first. Unlike Mexico, Guatemala has a large evangelical population and respects the Bible message.

In a park in downtown Guatemala City, a communist began insulting me and generally denying the existence of God as I spoke to a large crowd. He said I was probably a spy sent by the FBI or the CIA. I said I sure wished I was because the Baptists were about to starve me to death. He said, "I don't believe in God. I told you that ten times!" I replied, "Psalm 14:1 tells you eleven times you're a fool—he fool has said in his heart there is no God. Corrupt are they.'"

From Guatemala, I returned to Tapacula and then returned to Alway, Sinaloa, with Chole and Diana.

From there, I pulled the travel trailer to Durango, Durango, where John Wayne had made movies. Chole and Diana went ahead of me in a bus as the Mazatlan-Durango Highway was very dangerous. About halfway to Durango, I encountered the Espinaso del Diablo, a treacherous two-mile drop-off where the highway makes a sharp left at the bottom of a steep downgrade. I proceeded down this steep downgrade in first gear. I tried not to overbrake using the hydraulic handbrake so as not to deplete the hydraulic fluid. Down I went. As I neared the bottom of the steep grade near the two-mile cliff, I had my driver's door open and my foot outside. I was prepared to jump should my rig go over and down the steep cliff.

Well, I made it and turned left, but then I stalled in loose gravel going up an upgrade. I got out and flagged down a white VW bug. This was at night. The bug's driver set out flares, and with two brooms, we swept off the highway, and I proceeded to Durango where I was reunited with my family. Upon arriving at Durango, I had to change my clothes, especially my underwear.

In Durango, I collaborated with Bob Hawk, a Baptist missionary from North Carolina. We helped him there for three months.

On December 11, 1976, I was preaching in a park in front of the large Catholic cathedral in downtown Durango. This was the day of the Virgin of Guadalupe. As I preached the Bible, a man approached me. He was angry. He said he didn't like my preaching. He had a gun under his coat.

He asked me what I would do if he shot me. I replied, "I would die, go to heaven, and tell God that you did it, and you better watch out later as maybe an eighteen-wheeler might run over you." I walked away. Of course I was afraid. Thank God he didn't shoot.

From Durango, we decided to go to Jerez, Zacatecas, to start a Baptist mission. We rented a small building from a man and started inviting people over to listen to the Bible. Goats and chickens came into our building.

One problem there was the open water wells. I was always so afraid little Diana, age two, would fall in one. The folks around Jerez, Zacatecas, population fifty thousand, had money for cigarettes, booze, etc., but not enough money to board over these open water wells.

One night, a lady knocked on our travel trailer door. She was upset. She said her daughter was very sick and needed some medicine from the pharmacy. She said she had no money. I asked her where she went to church. She replied at the large Catholic church downtown. I asked her if she had asked the priest for help. She said no because he won't give me anything. We bought the medicine for her, and her daughter recovered.

I didn't stand on a street corner and indiscriminately pass out dollars like the proverbial ugly American. Many Americans flaunt their money and affluence in foreign countries—thus the book *The Ugly American*. We bought a blanket here, some medicine there, some help here, etc.

We began collaborating with a one Jesus Juarez, pastor of the First Baptist Church in downtown Zacatecas. He and I distributed literature all over Jerez and in many ranches some forty miles on each side of this town.

One of his missions near Jerez, Zacatecas, had a Russian pastor. He was formerly a communist in Mexicali.

There was much communist influence in central Mexico at that time, especially in the universities. This pastor and Jesus Juarez were good men but were ignorant of international politics. They actually believed the old evil Soviet Union was on the same par morally as the USA.

The Russian pastor needed financial support. I helped him with a monthly financial offering. I told Jesus to not tell him the money was from me. Later on, this Russian pastor was surprised and aghast that an American imperialist was the source of this money.

One evening, I was passing out tracts in a park in downtown Jerez next to the police station. When a small crowd formed, I began preaching. First ten, then twenty, then fifty, then one hundred, and then some two hundred people showed up. A gringo preaching the Bible was a real novelty to these people. The sermon evolved into religious debate. My Catholic friends gave their point of view, and I gave the biblical answer. This debate continued until two o'clock in the morning. The police hovered close by, listening and protecting me.

I was very energetic and aggressive in my preaching. Why be a sissy when one can be courageous, was my attitude! God protected me in spite of my immaturity.

Another interesting experience occurred at Chole's ranch. One day, I was playing baseball with the ranch's team. I noticed a one Manuel Gomez sitting behind the catcher to one side against the backstop. He was drinking, and he was angry with me. At times he cursed me. I asked him what his problem was. "You owe me $1,400, man," he said, and hit me in the posterior with a rock. I had taken his pregnant wife, eight months along, from Tijuana to Tarzana, California, just north of Los Angeles in 1975. The deal was for $800. Upon arriving at Tarzana, Manuel paid me absolutely nothing. I angrily broke every window in his car with a tire iron. "How much do I owe you Manuel?" I asked. "Fourteen hundred dollars," he replied. "How 'bout that $800 you promised me?" I asked. I replied that $1400 minus $800 is $600. "How 'bout I bring over the $600 tomorrow?" "Okay," he said.

Chole implored me not to go to this ranch alone. "The people at this ranch, Los Fierros, are violent," she said. The next day, I went to Manuel's ranch, gave him the $600, and returned to Chole's ranch. God had protected me again. I had not suffered (the rock on my hip) for righteousness sake, but for unrighteousness sake. Well, thereafter, I hoped that peace would reign in Chole's ranch.

Some of the people in this ranch, the Buena Vista, didn't appreciate me passing out Bible tracts. These folks at Buena Vista had not allowed in any non-Catholic people in the past. They had run off some Jehovah's Witnesses. One protestant missionary had dropped thousands of tracts out of a plane onto the ranch. Well, I told the folks if they got violent with me, they would have to deal with two hundred of Chole's relatives. They quieted down.

Every six months, I was required by Mexican law to leave Mexico for the United States to renew my six-months tourist card. We drove into McAllen, Texas, to do this. There I met a veteran missionary, Roy Johns, who headed a mission board. I joined his board.

Later he took over my church in Jerez so I could attend language school in Edinburg, Texas. My Spanish needed some honing up—both grammatically and phonetically. This was in the fall of 1978. I took an intensive two-year university-level, two-semester course in Spanish. I completed it in one semester.

This Rio Grande Bible Institute language school is one of the best language schools in the USA. The Mexican professors from Monterey, Mexico, almost drove me crazy. "George, conjugate this verb. George, give us the subjunctive of this other verb," etc. I was called on and targeted because I was the only missionary there who knew some Spanish and was the only one just off the mission field.

I struggled at first but began to jell during the middle and end of the semester. I graduated in December of 1978 with an A and delivered the graduation speech to the class.

In reference to Jerez, Mexico, and the work there, I felt I was a failure. I had preached to so many people. I had distributed so many tracts, and I had worked so hard, yet I had seen little fruit. A few years later, I was amazed to learn that several evangelical churches had sprung up all over that town. God's word will not return void (Isaiah 55:11).

From the Rio Grande Valley, we returned to San Diego with plans to start a work in Chole's hometown of Tijuana. On the west side of Tijuana, we rented a building about a mile from Chole's home. I then met a preacher from Monterey, Mexico. He agreed to be the pastor.

We started a Baptist mission. It flourished. In one year, we were running two hundred people. There were many conversions and baptisms.

Of course, the devil never sleeps. One day while picking up pastor Eliseo's coat, out fell a Tijuana bank book revealing fifty thousand pesos. Our agreement at the outset was a certain designated amount of money would be given to Eliseo monthly by some churches and a missionary in San Diego. When I inquired about this to Eliseo, a second preacher from another church intervened, butted in, and in general, caused an argument and an uproar. After repeated requests that this second preacher leave Chole's building (it was in her name), I used physical force to remove him. I thought that was better than involving the Mexican police who loved *mordida* (bribes).

These two preachers filed a civil suit of $4,000 against Chole and myself in a federal agency, and then put charges of *lesiones* (felony assault) against me.

While discussing the civil suit at the Judicial State Police Office, one of the detectives told me, "George, serious charges, *lesiones*, have been filed against you. Just go out the back door now with your wife and go quickly over to California to avoid arrest." Even these non-Christian lawmen saw how phony and unfair these charges were.

Chole was my agent the following year between the federal agency and myself. She almost had a nervous breakdown. By the way, the civil case was dismissed two years later. The federal officials told Eliseo and the other preacher if they wanted money to get a job!

Being open and aboveboard, I told my supporting churches around the USA about these problems. I should have just said, "Pray for us as the devil is fighting us." I was too frank and honest. I lost half of my financial support, which wasn't much. I guess some churches thought I was running in the bars in Tijuana.

So after much prayer and thought, Chole and I decided to no longer ask churches for financial support. That is, we would no longer approach churches for support unless invited first. If God wanted us to stay in Mexico, he would provide the finances. If not, God had other plans for us.

When sufficient money did not come in, we moved to Mission, Texas, in the Rio Grande Valley. I started working for a living. This was in 1980. We did retain $5,000 of the money I had earned illegally. The rest was spent on our expenses and given away during the previous four years.

In McAllen, Texas, I applied for a dishwashing job at a Chinese restaurant. Since I felt I was overqualified for the job, I kind of played dumb during the interview. "George, why do you think you can do this job?" they asked. "I'm the fastest gun in the west," I replied. Laughing, they hired me.

Running that dishwashing machine was so difficult I could hardly stand up when I got off work. I decided to go into business for myself.

With some capital, I started buying new radios, portable phonograph players, Walkman stereos, etc., from some Jewish wholesalers in downtown McAllen. We decided to sell them at the South Twenty-Third Flea Market in McAllen. This place only had used-junk dealers. We immediately started doing good business there.

One hot-selling item was the refill pencil with lead fillers. I started buying them from a large wholesaler on Main Street. The best seller was one with a fruit scent.

I decided to go around the middle man and directly to the importer. I played like I was hustling aluminum cans in the alley behind my Main Street supplier. I was actually looking for the importer's address and name on the discarded boxes in the dumpsters. The store owner asked me what I was doing. "Looking for aluminum cans," I said. He gave me four or five cans. I found the importer's address—a company in Elizabeth or in Fort Lee, New Jersey. Chole later made a five-thousand-dollar sale off these scented refill pencils to a retail store in Hidalgo, Texas.

We bought a cracker box mobile home in Mission, Texas, for $1,500, and began working in various flea markets in Mercedes, Donna, San Juan, and Rio Grande City.

We developed a route in the Rio Grande Valley, and I began selling small convenience stores merchandise at wholesale prices. I especially sold hundreds and hundreds of Panasonic and Rayovac batteries.

I recall buying a large container of twenty-thousand pairs of jelly shoes from New York. When the Rubic Cube craze started in 1982, I sold thousands and thousands.

Due to the 1984 devaluation of the Mexican peso, we decided to move to San Antonio, Texas. After staying there nine months, we moved back to San Diego, California.

After almost going broke there in a small stand in San Ysidro, we hit pay dirt. I rented a store in Tecate, California, in east San Diego County some few feet from the Mexican border with Tecate, Mexico. Ours was the only retail store selling general merchandise in this town of two hundred people. Seventy-five thousand people lived across the border in Tecate, Mexico.

We rented from one Mike Skinner who had founded and ran a large grocery store next door. Mike sold tons of beer at his store. You've heard, of course, of Tecate beer. Their brewery is in Tecate, Mexico. I think an AA club was located every ten blocks in Tecate, Mexico.

One day, after observing the devastating effects booze was causing the local folks, I challenged Mike Skinner. "Mike, I said, every time I win one soul to Christ, you send me fifty drunks!" Mike got good and mad. He was six feet four inches and 250 pounds. He looked like Tom Selleck.

Later, he came in my store. He was angry. I told him if he hit me, I would put him in jail for six months. He backed off.

A few weeks later, here he came. I told Chole, "Now I'm going to lose my teeth." In my store he came. He shocked me. He asked me, "What do we learn from Jesus's death on the cross." "Well," I gulped and said, "how about forgiveness? Why don't you and I smoke the peace pipe and present to each other an olive branch." He agreed.

What a miracle! Not too many wealthy grocery-chain owners in Southern California talk about Jesus's forgiveness. Mike's family owned two large grocery stores—one in El Centro and one in Calexico.

We stayed there in Tecate, California from 1986 to 1993. In 1993, my contract with Mike's company, T. C. Worthy, expired. Payless Shoes came in, doubled the size of the store, and leased it for $10,000 a month.

We and Mike separated friends. I bought him a nice Bible. He surprised us when he told us he was listening to a Christian program on the radio. He said he had invited Jesus into his heart.

Mike had a $500,000 home in El Cajon. He owned a half-million-dollar motor home. He had two or three handsome children and a beautiful wife. However, I think his drinking problem done him in. He once wrecked his motorcycle on the dangerous Highway 94 between Tecate and El Cajon while intoxicated. How sad! In 1994, when we were in Texas, Mike picked up a pistol and blew his brains out! Maybe if protestant and Catholic Christians did not sell booze, these tragedies might not happen.

In 1993, we moved back to Palacios, Texas, on the Gulf Coast. We started buying merchandise in Houston and selling in the open air in different towns. In over ten years, I opened stores in Port Lavaca, Bay City, Edna, Victoria, Mission, Raymondville, Freer, Alice, Beeville, Alpine, and finally stopped and planted our roots in Fort Stockton, Texas, in 2003.

Chole told me I was unstable. "Not so," I replied. I told her I was a stable traveling salesman. Actually, we jumped around for ten years trying to find a place where we could get ahead and make a profit. We barely eked out a living in these other towns.

In Fort Stockton, we rented a store from Ruben Falcon, Sr. We started doing well because Fort Stockton is a long way from competitors and the big cities. In addition, being in the oil-rich Permian Basin of west Texas helped.

Ruben was from Mexico. He was patient, kind, and gentle. He ran a fine restaurant, La Bienvenidos, in Fort Stockton. He began having marital problems with his wife, who was the cook. He began drinking heavily. His wife and son cut him off financially at the restaurant.

One day, I asked Ruben a personal question. "Ruben," I said, "if you died today, are you 100 percent sure your soul would go to heaven?" "Well, I'm a Catholic," he answered. "I didn't ask you your denominational preference. I asked you where you were going if you died today." "I'm trying to do the best I can," he said. "That's commendable," I said, "but the best you and I can do is not good enough. You can't fly to heaven by your bootstraps or your shoestrings. You need Jesus." "I believe in the Virgin, the saints, and have my priest," Ruben said. I replied, "The only Virgin, saint, or priest that could save us and truly absolve our sins is Virgin Jesus, Saint Jesus, and Priest Jesus." I told him this is what the bible teaches. I told him we can't be saved by being sweet little protestants or nice little Catholics because we are sinners—a fallen race. I stated we haven't always been sweet and nice. I mentioned our salvation is not in a brick protestant building or in a majestic Catholic cathedral, but that salvation is much higher than earthly buildings. I said, "Ruben, salvation is in Jesus Christ and in him alone."

On December 2, 2008, Ruben Falcon, Sr., hung himself to death in his home in Fort Stockton. What a shame! People think by killing themselves they will escape life's problems, but how about the judgment of Almighty God that comes after death?

Two landlords of mine committed suicide within fourteen years of each other. "Hey, anybody out there reading this want to be my landlord? Want to rent me a store?"

CONCLUSION

1. The inconsistency of our federal and state insanity laws. What the courts are doing is hospitalizing sane criminals and incarcerating insane patients in prisons. They make many mistakes. They gave me a license to steal.

2. Psychiatrists and psychologists are only human. They err. I don't believe psychiatry is an exact science. I believe Sigmund (sick-mind) Freud was a fraud in many ways. He stated that the two strongest drives in the human being are self-preservation and the sex drive. This unconverted, unregenerate, non-Christian psychiatrist was blind and unaware of a third drive—the drive or desire to love and please God.

    I believe Jung taught a bunch of junk. James rightly said a large majority of mental patients in mental institutions would not be there if they could get rid of their guilt. Hey, try Jesus! "Come now, and let us reason together, saith the Lord: though your sins be as scarlet, they shall be as white as snow; though they are red like crimson, they shall be as wool" (Isaiah 1:18). Try Psalm 103:12, "As far as the east is from the west, so far hath he removed our transgressions from us." Micah 17:19 says, "He will turn again, he will have compassion upon us; he will subdue our inequities; and thou wilt cast all their sins into the depths of the sea." "For I will be merciful to their unrighteousness, and their sins and inequities will I remember no more" (Hebrews 8:12). First Timothy 1:15 says, "This is a faithful saying, and worthy of all acceptation, that Christ Jesus came into the world to save sinners; of whom I am chief. Mental patients, psychiatrists, psychologists, and all people should read and believe these verses!"

Now psychiatrists and psychologists do some good. They can inject a violent inmate or patient in the rear end with a tranquilizer to calm him down. However, I believe the American public has been sold a bill of goods by this profession. Are you aware these gurus of peace have the highest suicide rate among professionals? They have conned America with their techniques, methods, counsel, psychotherapy, psychoanalysis, etc., yet they jump out of windows more than any other profession.

Even Dear Abby suggests we seek out a licensed, professional therapist. This humanist almost never suggests seeking out a spiritual man of God.

Yes, these pseudo-doctors will put you on their couches at $300 to $400 per hour. They'll ask you about your relationship with your mother and father when you were a child. They counsel some married couples to "play the field"—to strike up a new romance (adultery), to snap out of their doldrums and depression.

I believe many of these quacks get into this field of employment because of their own insecurities. Calling someone else crazy boosts their own ego. Of course, money is also involved. Pastoring a Christian church or working as a Christian counselor doesn't pay very well.

A good, godly bible-believing pastor will counsel one with serious problems for hours and hours at all times of the day or night, free of charge!

The premise of psychiatry is wrong at the outset. Most in this profession do not believe in God. They are fools (Psalm 53:1)! If a Christian prays to God, he's hallucinating. If God speaks to a believer through the scriptures or through the impressions of the Holy Spirit indwelling him, he is suffering illusions. Paul, the apostle of Jesus Christ, asked a question in 1 Corinthians 1:20: Where is the wise? Where is the scribe? Where is the disputer of this world? Answer: In hell burning!

These people deny the existence of sin, which is the breaking of the Ten Commandments. First John 3:4b says, "For sin is the transgression of the law." Romans 3:23 states, "For all have sinned and come short of the glory of God." They call sin mistakes, a weakness, an environmental factor, repressed desires, etc. They deny the existence of inherited sin, that we are all born sinners. Psalm 58:3 says, "The wicked are estranged from the womb; they go astray as soon as they be born, speaking lies." Psalm 51:5 states, "Behold, I was shapen in inequity; and in sin did my mother conceive me." Ephesians 2:3b says, "And were by nature the children of wrath, even as others, referring to us all." Most in this profession are agnostics, atheists, freethinkers, or humanists, like many Americans. Maybe this is why most Americans have bought this unbiblical nonsense!

3.   I'm for prisons. I was a volunteer Christian worker in three south Texas state prisons in the nineties. Dangerous and violent people who behave like animals need to be caged to protect society. However, incarceration does not change human nature—the human heart. Christ does! "Therefore, if any man be in Christ, he is a new creature: old things are passed away; behold, all things are become new" (2 Corinthians 5:17).

The main goal of our wardens and our guards in prisons is for the prison to be peaceful, tranquil, and secure. I believe most wardens and prison employees do not care if the inmates are rehabilitated or not. They just want a quiet and secure prison. They want their job to be easy. If an inmate dies and goes to hell forever, who cares? After all, if all the inmates go straight, the warden and the prison employees lose their jobs in these human warehouses.

A notable example: I was a volunteer Christian worker in the nineties in the Lopez Velarde state prison in Edinburg, Texas. About one-third or more of the prison population converted to Christ while I was preaching there. This was between 1996 and 1999. The inmates identified with me as I had also served hard time.

A really good Baptist chaplain invited me to speak to the inmates there. I met him at a Baptist church in Weslaco, Texas.

He would warn me, "George, be careful today. The new lady chaplain is on duty. She's real liberal and a real fanatic for prison rules." When she was not present, he would tell me, "Sick 'em, George! Sock it to them!" In my sermon, I would ask the inmates if they were a man or a mouse. I would ask them if they were chickens. If they indicated they were men, I would challenge them to come forward, renounce their criminal careers, repent of sin, and accept Jesus as Savior. I preached hard! I would say, "Some of you think you're tough so you hit a seventy-five-year-old grandmother in the head with a tire iron. If you're really tough, a real man, and fearless, I challenge you to come up front right now before all your buddies and get right with God. Don't be chicken. *Putt, putt, putt, putt-up,*" I would say, as I imitated a chicken.

Hundreds of inmates converted to Christ in this Texas Department of Criminal Justice prison of 2000. Some contacted me after their release.

Well, the new liberal chaplain told me she didn't raise her voice when preaching to the inmates. I replied that I did. Isaiah 58:1 says, "Cry aloud, spare not, lift up thy voice like a trumpet, and show my people there transgression, and the house of Jacob their sins."

When some of the inmates, the religious kind, complained to her about my preaching, she called me in on the carpet. "George, you must be lower-key. You're too strong." I told her if she began to censor my sermons, I would leave. Her interference continued and I left. Some of the inmates cried.

As I said, I believe most of our criminal justice system do not want criminals to rehabilitate. I believe most prison employees do not want to work themselves out of a job.

The self-preservation of the prison employees takes precedence over the welfare and future of the inmates.

In the first part of this book, I didn't describe my adventures—my crimes, etc., as a "how-to-do crime" book. I'm ashamed and embarrassed about the years I was a bum and a criminal. This is one reason I have waited so many years to write this. I have tried to make this book interesting and entertaining. After all, had I written about the mating habits of the Monarch butterfly, I doubt you would have read it. The Rev. Jack Hyles, now deceased, who had the largest Baptist church in America in Hammond, Indiana, during the 1970s, 1980s, and 1990s said a boring sermon preached by a boring preacher is not spiritual.

The devil never sleeps. The Bible teaches there is a terrible, sinister, and evil force in this world behind all the murder, chaos, injustice, and suffering. Second Corinthians 4:4 says, "In whom the God of this world hath blinded the minds of them which believe not, lest the light of the glorious gospel of Christ, who is the image of God, should shine unto them." If the devil can't get you in one area, he'll try something else, such as money, fame, power, popularity, booze, drugs, a promiscuous lifestyle, intellectual attainment, or phony-baloney, man-made, unbiblical religion. Christ, the light of the world, has come not to condemn us but to save us—to bring us out of satanic darkness into his light.

In closing, may I say my prayer is for the reader, regardless of his or her status or station in life, to accept precious Jesus into his or her life now by faith and repentance. If the reader is a believer, may this book draw you closer to sweet Jesus, the only hope for fallen mankind.

2 Thess. 3:1 – "Brethren, Pray for us."

GEORGE SOLEDAD &DENI PITTS –
MISSIONARIES TO MEXICO

If you wish to contact Mr. Pitts, address is below:

George Pitts
610 West Dickinson Blvd
Fort Stockton, TX 79735

ssification Form 2
ev. January 1939

UNITED STATES DEPARTMENT OF JUSTICE
BUREAU OF PRISONS

MEDICAL CENTER FOR FEDERAL PRISONERS
Springfield, Missouri

SPECIAL PROGRESS REPORT

Committed Name   PITTS, George T.   Reg. No.   P-470-H   Date   Apr. 25, 1962

REPORT OF NEUROPSYCHIATRIC STAFF EXAMINATION – 2-15-62

The Neuropsychiatric Staff met today and reviewed the records and recent Report of Neuropsychiatric Examination on George T. Pitts, Reg. No. P-470-H. The patient was also examined at some length.

The Neuropsychiatric Staff noted that the patient is a 24-year old white male currently incarcerated at the Medical Center under provisions of Title 18, Section 4246, USC, charged with interstate transportation of forged securities. The Staff was aware that the patient had been recommended for state hospitalization in his state of residence by the Civil Rights Division in view of the manifold evidence surrounding this patient's crime and mental illness.

When the patient was examined by the Neuropsychiatric Staff, the Staff noted that the patient appeared much as described in the recent Report of Neuropsychiatric Examination by Dr. Dickinson and the patient again went to some lengths to convince the members of the Staff as to his degree of mental health. The Staff noted that the patient was unrealistic in his attempts to solve his current problem and that the thinking demonstrated by the patient was definitely of a schizophrenic nature.

RECOMMENDATIONS: The Neuropsychiatric Staff continues to concur in the diagnosis of Schizophrenic Reaction, Chronic Undifferentiated Type and is of the opinion that the patient continues to be unable to understand the nature of the charges pending against him or to assist counsel in his defense.

APPROVED: R. Eugene Holemon
R. EUGENE HOLEMON, M. D.
Acting Chief, Psychiatric Service

JOHN DICKINSON, M. D.
Staff Psychiatrist

JD:rg
3-1-62

Staff Members present: Drs. Stamm, Holemon and Dickinson.

COMMITTEE RECOMMENDATIONS:
April 25, 1962

The classification committee recommends that efforts be continued to arrange hospitalization in his state of residence.
The committee further recommends that this report be referred to the Bureau of Prisons and the Committing Court for informational purposes and that this patient continue his present psychiatric treatment program.

63

Classification Form 1b
Rev. January 1955

UNITED STATES DEPARTMENT OF JUSTICE
BUREAU OF PRISONS

Page ____

CLASSIFICATION STUDY
(Continued)

Committed Name   PITTS, George T.   Register Number   P-170-H

REPORT OF NEUROPSYCHIATRIC EXAMINATION (READMISSION)

I. REASON FOR COMMITMENT: This patient is a 25-year old white male who was originally sent to the Medical Center on June 13, 1961 under provisions of Title 18, Section 4244, USC, for a mental evaluation as to the patient's competency to stand trial on charges of interstate transportation of forged securities. Following initial evaluation and recommendation of the Neuropsychiatric Staff, the patient was returned to court on September 5, 1961 where he was adjudicated incompetent to stand trial and was returned to the Medical Center on December 6, 1961 under provisions of Title 18, Section 4246, USC.

II. SOURCES OF INFORMATION: The patient who can be considered only moderately reliable and the institutional records which are adequate.

III. FAMILY & PERSONAL HISTORY: For details of the patient's family and personal history, the reader is kindly referred to this examiner's previous Report of Neuro-psychiatric Examination on the patient's initial commitment under Section 4244, dated August 17, 1961.

IV. PRESENT SITUATION: Following the patient's examination and consideration before the Neuropsychiatric Staff on his commitment here as Reg. No. 0-411-H, the Neuropsychiatric Staff made the recommendation that because of a severe degree of mental illness, the Staff was of the opinion that the patient was not able to consult with his lawyer with a reasonable degree of rational understanding and did not have a rational or factual understanding of the proceedings pending against him. The patient was returned to court and shortly after his arrival, was examined by Dr. William B. McGrath, consulting psychiatrist and it was Dr. McGrath's opinion that "at the time of commission of the alleged act, it is my opinion that Mr. Pitts had an active mental disease (schizophrenia). It is my further opinion that this mental disease rendered him incapable of distinguishing right from wrong or of knowing the nature and consequences of his act. Secondly, the clouded state of that interval, persisting almost to the present, would surely impair his ability to understand pro-ceedings or aid counsel in his defense at this time. Too, the residuals of the schizophrenic illness presently dull his entire capacity to understand or heed. Lastly, he is still certifiable for regular commitment as a mentally ill person; i.e., he is potentially dangerous to himself and others by reason of his mental condition (chronic schizophrenia). However, the disease is presently in partial remission. Hence, his institutionalization at this time does not appear urgent or mandatory to this examiner -- especially if his relatives are willing to provide some supervision and support. There is, however, some probability that the patient's schizophrenic illness will become active again in the future and further hospital-ization will be required". The court for the District of Arizona took all of these recommendations into consideration and ordered that the patient be recommitted to the Medical Center under provisions of Title 18, Section 4246. Also apparently at the same time, a petition was filed with the Civil Rights Division to get the charges pending against the patient dismissed contingent on his admission to a mental hospital in his state of residence. This procedure was carried forward and it was officially recommended to the Bureau of Prisons that steps be made to institute hospitalization

Classification Form 1b
Rev. January 1965

UNITED STATES DEPARTMENT OF JUSTICE
BUREAU OF PRISONS

Page   2

CLASSIFICATION STUDY
(Continued)

Committed Name   PITTS, George T.   Register Number   P-470-H

in his state of residence as charges pending against him would be dropped if state hospital care for the patient could be arranged. Consequently, procedures are being instituted with the State of Texas to obtain a state hospital commitment for this patient.

V. COURSE IN HOSPITAL: Since the patient's return to the Medical Center, he has maintained an adequate adjustment living on a semi-closed ward for psychiatric patients. It was the opinion of the Psychiatric Staff that the patient did not require this secure housing but because there were no openings on the patient's previous ward of residence, it was decided to move him to his current ward of residence rather than to hold him in the Admission and Orientation Unit for an inordinate amount of time. The patient has been receiving average to above average work reports on his job in the Educational Department and has been attempting to convince everyone of his current state of mental health.

VI. OUTLINE OF MENTAL STATUS: The patient entered the examining room in a superficially affable and pleasant way and tried to be extremely ingratiating with this examiner. The patient seemed to be in excellent physical health and his appearance was appropriate concerning his facial expression, gait, mannerisms and dress. However, the patient immediately launched into a grossly over-determined narrative which was intended to impress this examiner with the patient's current mental clarity and his accurate knowledge concerning the nature of the offense with which he is currently charged. This was an extremely superficial relating of several facts which had undoubtedly been told to the patient by those who had come in contact with him over the course of his time here at the Medical Center and at court. The patient stated that he had remembered all of these things all along and that he knew everything which had gone on. The patient was apparently trying to simulate mental health and when he was confronted with some of his past bizarre episodes and past statements that he did not remember certain things, he would stop in his speech, look blank for a few seconds then seemingly pull himself together and continue on in his narrative as if the examiner had not even spoken to him.

Much of the patient's stream of thought was concerned in expressing to the examiner how well he was feeling now, that he was sleeping better now and that he wanted very much to be found competent so that he could return to court to stand trial even though he might be found guilty and given some penitentiary time. This was construed to be a grossly irrational and illogical approach to the patient's problem by the patient rather than a display of the patient's inate honesty. He continued to emphasize how well he remembered everything which had happened to him but it was quite obvious as the tenses of his verbs changed from clause to clause that he really does not remember very much at all.

The patient in his currently superficial relationship is blocking out a great deal of meaningful material and using primarily defenses of denial, rationalization, minimization and evasion. Currently there is no gross delusionary content to the patient's thought and there are no apparent hallucinations. The patient is both circumstantial and tangential on occasion, exhibits poor goal direction and has loosened associations. On the surface, he looks the picture of health but if one but scratches the surface, one sees a wealth of residual schizophrenic thought disorder and emotional conflict which is the true picture of the patient's condition at this time.

Classification Form 1b
Rev. January 1965

UNITED STATES DEPARTMENT OF JUSTICE
BUREAU OF PRISONS

CLASSIFICATION STUDY
(Continued)

Page ___3___

Committed Name   PITTS, George T.   Register Number   P-470-H

VII. DIAGNOSIS: 000-x26 Schizophrenic Reaction, chronic Undifferentiated Type,
with paranoid and catatonic features, in current remission,
as manifested by a history of both visual and auditory hallucinations, delusions of persecution and grandeur, religious
preoccupation, mutism, difficulties in maintaining or establish-
ing interpersonal relations, ambivalence, autism, the presence
of obsessive compulsive defense mechanisms as a reintegrative
mechanism toward mental health, manifold fears, free-floating
anxiety, gross disturbances in intellection, affective splitting
and currently a sincere but ineffective effort to simulate
mental health with additional unrealistic ideas toward meeting
his current life's situation.

JOHN DICKINSON, M. D.
Staff Psychiatrist

JD:rg
3-1-62

66

IN THE UNITED STATES DISTRICT COURT

FOR THE DISTRICT OF ARIZONA

UNITED STATES OF AMERICA,

            Plaintiff,

      vs.

  GEORGE T. PITTS

          Defendant .

Criminal No. C-15776 Phx.

ORDER FOR DISMISSAL

      Pursuant to Rule 48(a) of the Federal Rules of Criminal Procedure and by leave of court endorsed hereon, the United States Attorney for the District of Arizona hereby dismisses the ___indictment___
(Indictment, Information, Complaint) against the above named Defendant .

United States Attorney

By TOM KARAS
Assistant U. S. Attorney

Violation: 18 USC 2314 - Interstate Transportation of Forged Securities

Leave of court is granted for the filing of the foregoing dismissal, and it is ordered that the defendant be forthwith released.

United States District Judge

Date: May 6, 1963

FILED

MAY 6 1963

67

ABOUT THE AUTHOR

George Pitts was born in the Panhandle of Texas in 1937, in a family of cotton sharecroppers. His father later became a commercial fisherman on the Texas Gulf Coast at Palacios, Texas. This was between 1944 and 1952.

Due to his father's drunkenness and violence, Pitts was placed in Buckner Orphan's Home in Dallas, Texas, in 1949. He left in 1954.

Perhaps this rough and unstable childhood contributed to Pitts' criminal career later in life.

While passing out business cards in Zacatecas, Mexico, in 1975, seeking people to smuggle into California from Tijuana, Pitts became very sick and converted to Christ. He returned to California and served three months in jail, attended a Baptist church, and later went to Mexico as a missionary. Running low on money, he returned to Texas where he has operated stores for thirty-six years.

CPSIA information can be obtained
at www.ICGtesting.com
Printed in the USA
FSOW01n0641291116
27820FS